DATE DUE

DEC 01 '90			
JUL 31 '92			
JUL 31 '92			
GAYLORD			PRINTED IN U.S.A.

GOD AND OTHER GODS

BOOKS BY ETHEL SABIN SMITH

God and Other Gods
The Dynamics of Aging
Passports at Seventy
A Furrow Deep and True

GOD AND OTHER GODS

*Essays in Perspective
on Persisting Religious Problems*

Ethel Sabin Smith, Ph.D.

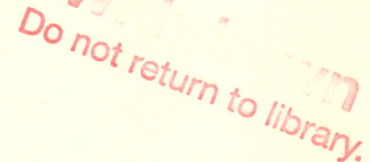

Andrew S. Thomas Memorial Library
MORRIS HARVEY COLLEGE, CHARLESTON, W. VA.

An Exposition-University Book
EXPOSITION PRESS   NEW YORK

EXPOSITION PRESS, INC.

50 Jericho Turnpike, Jericho, New York 11753

FIRST EDITION

© 1973 by Ethel Sabin Smith. All rights reserved, including the right of reproduction in whole or in part in any form except for short quotations in critical essays and reviews. Manufactured in the United States of America.

SBN 0-682-47619-6

To

My Brothers
with Affection

Contents

	PREFACE: To Whom It Does Concern	ix
I	Judgment Day à la Mode	3
II	Assorted Angels	13
III	"Turn but a Stone, and Start a Wing"	25
IV	The Food Mystique	35
V	The Greatest News Story in the Memory of Man	47
VI	The Mortal Gods	56
VII	Pattern	67
VIII	Half Gods	80
IX	Needed: a Devil	92
X	Gadgets, Gestures and the Calendar	103
XI	Monstrous Gods	117
XII	Pious Cloaks	128
XIII	Women, Adored and Abhorred	138
XIV	"Mirror, Mirror, Tell Me True"	150
XV	Twin Sisters	166
XVI	Postscript	179
	INDEX	181

Preface:
To Whom It Does Concern

These loosely related essays could be called commentaries, except that "commentaries" sounds forbidding and erudite. These essays are less scholarly than that. They are merely comments in a somewhat conversational tone, addressed not to accomplished scholars but to young students with questions.

They are also meant to be *apologia*, or defense statements, for the sort of traditional education that is currently under attack as irrelevant to the needs of our time. I have a fierce faith in the profound and unqualified relevancy of traditional education, and I believe that the survival of civilization depends on it at its best. The future of mankind is, at the moment, dark and uncertain. The only light we can throw upon it comes from the past. We need to utilize that past, every aspect of it, to prevent our children's children from living in the dark ages of a possible future.

I am not out of sympathy with change in education. It is necessary. Thus, I welcome the demand for ethnic studies in higher education, as long as each area of ethnic study is recognized as the fragment it is and viewed in the vast mosaic of human, as opposed to racial, history. Just as each individual is stronger, happier, and more effective when he takes his place in life in full knowledge of and pride in the family he represents and the country of which he is a son, just so racial awareness adds to his stature. Few individuals are able to go beyond this point, but they, I believe, are the truly educated, who glory in their humanity and conduct themselves with the dignity and authority becoming a member of the human race. Was Goethe the first of modern men to claim the title of "Citizen of the World"? Only to men without scientific background and the training of a liberal education can man's slow climb from slime to his present estate seem "irrelevant" information, lacking, for example, the immediacy of knowing how to capture the markets of the world with a new cosmetic.

The study of fairy tales and myths, of dead religions, and of the false beliefs of peoples and civilizations no longer extant is high on the list of useless things the reformers wish to sweep out of the curricula of the functional education they plan for the morrow. It is the prevailing mood that history, unless it can be used to further a present project or enhance a pressure group, should receive academic burial. Who cares about the Hittites? Has anybody in the picket line a Hittite grandfather?

The iconoclasts of learning are today asking why we should study old religions. "By Jove!" may be a common exclamation, but who cares about a Roman god who never existed anyway? To waste time on the study of the Stoic idea of world harmony or, worse still, on the downright absurdities of the Cynics seems to the impatient reformers of university education an obvious anachronism. They are, however, eager to study Zen Buddhism, blissfully unaware of its Cynic overtones and the parallels of Stoic thinking in this modern cult.

This argument, of course, is the gist of this book. I am trying to say to this generation that the past lives on in the present. Edith Hamilton wrote of it eloquently as "The Ever-living Past." Just as we still carry in our blood the brine of the distant seas from which our progenitors emerged, so modern thought holds primitive thought encapsulated in its stream. "Encapsulated" is not really the right word. The past is the very essence of the stream. Often history alone can reveal the meaning of what is contemporary. The magnificent service of institutions of higher education is not only to explore and discover, not only to conserve and to treasure, but to set in perspective, namely, to teach what they hold in trust.

We can nourish our bodies with instant coffee and instant oatmeal, but instant knowledge remains a contradiction in terms. Yet the crash educational programs that the rebelling generation demands and assumes it is competent to inaugurate, supervise, and administer would of necessity consist mainly of instant ideas that float about on the surface of our times.

This combination of lack of perspective and audacity is not a new phenomenon in young people. Longfellow noted it in his "Ode on the Fiftieth Reunion" of his class at Bowdoin College. He wrote rather admiringly of the "audacious feet" of young people willing to ascend a ladder "leaning on a cloud." Socrates came face to face with it in ancient Athens, when he stopped the son of an old friend on the street. The boy was hurrying to a magistrate to accuse his father of impiety. "What is impiety?" Socrates asked; he found the boy did not really know but felt it a duty to inform on his father anyway.

Gods and Other Gods, while not a history of religion, is an attempt to set certain persisting religious matters in ethnic and historical perspective. I am concerned not so greatly with the idea of God, as with the natures of the many gods men have worshipped in what Professor Atkins so aptly called, "The Procession of the Gods."

Just as we frame pictures to see them better by setting them apart from their immediate environment, so we need to isolate beliefs about matters important to us such as immortality, prayer, and faith healing in order to see them objectively. Such a separation from their usual context takes place when they are framed by a religious context different from one's own and perhaps remote in time and place.

I know of nothing more relevant to human need than answers to the questions that each generation of men asks anew, such as "Who am I?" "What is my relationship to the universe?" "What can I hope?" "What must I fear?" These are the very questions from which religions arise. To sort out some of the historical answers and to frame them for easy viewing is the object of this study. To this end I bring together within the limits of each chapter the insights diverse religions of the world have offered for each of several selected problems that vex us today.

To take a simple example, though in this case one that does not involve a highly vexatious or burning problem: How have the various ancient peoples of the world reported the flood, which probably did occur, and more particularly what meaning did they attach to it? Was it to punish men for sin, or did it reflect strife among the gods with man the victim but not the cause?

Authentic information about Noah and his ark may admittedly have little relevance to current issues, although we must admit that entirely fictional legendary events may have distinct impact, but insofar as the religions of the world have largely shaped man's ideas of justice, truth, and the good life, a man ignorant of religions is handicapped in his thinking.

Concepts of "the good life," derived from the religion to which he is born, usually begin early to control a man's life, inherited as they are with his mother tongue. They may be uncritically held. If so, in a crisis they fail him. When he discards them, he finds life suddenly meaningless. In the ensuing crash what he most needs is not a new religion, but the knowledge of many religions to save his values when he loses his faith.

These studies in perspective aim to bring to bear on a few vital issues the thinking of many men of the far distant past and of the present, writers in remote lands and in the home-town daily paper, ideas of philosophers and of humble neighbors. The book does not seek to indoctrinate. It does seek to enlighten by drawing on findings of contemporary scientists as well as ancient seers. Not only from the Bible but also from the Koran, from the Bhagavad-Gita and from the sayings of Confucius, men have learned and still can learn about the issues of life.

One is able to see a concept in a new way when one compares it with either a similar or a very different formulation in other great religions. For example: "In the beginning was the word" gains depth of meaning when one compares it with the Stoic concept of "Logos" or lays gently beside it the sacred Sanskrit word "Om," symbol to Hindus of Brahma or God.

Primitive chants and recently deciphered Sumerian hymns, Egyptian incantations, the Zoroastrian literature of the Gathas, poetry of the Rig-Veda and sutras from Buddhist texts, the Upanishads and the poems of our Quaker poet Whittier, all offer answers. The answers differ, but they are serious answers, worth noting, to the gravely insistent questions men have always asked and will ask anew.

Young people bent on repudiating the liberal-arts tradition of education that nourished their fathers, who spurn as useless the humanism of the recent past, may, hopefully, learn to read again, and read not only their contemporary literature of dissent, with its inevitable bias, but read also what heretics and heroes long dead engraved on pillars or entrusted to papyrus or wrote in characters strange to us on tablets and on scrolls. This, in translation, the young with open minds may miraculously purchase in paperbacks at the corner bookstore.

Man alone, among all the mammals, can transport into his present day the content of all former days. He does it by the various arts, by writing, and by speech. Without the precious burden he has brought with him as a wanderer in time, he would remain animal, but not human. A human being at his best is a very precious thing.

This book does not seek to establish or to destroy any particular religion. If it manages to throw light on problems that, for the most part, religions have in common, it will have fulfilled its purpose. Above all, it is saying to young people who are religiously perplexed—if you learn to doubt wisely, you will discover much that is precious that you may keep.

GOD AND OTHER GODS

What is all science then,
But pure religion seeking everywhere
The true commandments, and through many forms
The eternal power that binds all worlds in one?
It is man's age-long struggle to draw near
His maker—learn his thought, discern his laws
A boundless task, in whose infinitude,
As in the unfolding light and law of love
Abides our hope, and our eternal joy.

ALFRED NOYES

CHAPTER I

Judgment Day a la Mode

In our culture, Judgment Day may be used to refer to two different events, one personal, one cosmic. It may refer to the soul's confrontation with a celestial judge or with its maker immediately following the body's death, and the judgment given may admit the soul to heaven or banish it to eternal torment. Or it may refer to what is often thought of as the end of the world, or Doom's Day, when the universe itself will be destroyed by a cleansing fire.

In the sacred books of the world religions, there are somewhat different accounts of each Judgment Day, but interesting agreement also as to the purpose each serves. As the Bible says: "Be certain that your sins will find you out."

Students of religion have been able to produce eloquent proof that religion arises out of fear and that the gods man has worshipped through the ages are the inventions of his frantic imaginings, in order to make himself at home in an indifferent universe. It is aside from my purpose in this book to inquire into the matter. However, in the study of beliefs about Judgment Day one is brought to an important observation about human nature. One cannot fail to be impressed with the stubbornness of man's conviction that "in the end justice is served." Those religions that lack a Judgment Day have something just as effective, the ineluctable law of "Karma."

Bayard Taylor was not inventing a new notion but putting into rhyming words an idea old and familiar to all of us when he wrote: "Till the sun grows old and the stars are cold and the leaves of the Judgment Book unfold."

With no effort we understood and agreed with John Fiske when he wrote: "The United States was bounded on the North by Aurora Borealis, on the South by the procession of the equinoxes, on the East by primeval chaos, and on the West by the Day of Judgment." What is the history of the idea of Judgment Day? If we journey backwards in time to ancient Egypt, we can find in the Egyptian Book of the Dead and in sculptured ruins and ancient inscriptions much evidence of the importance for Egypt of a personal Judgment Day. The Egyptians believed that at a man's death his "ka" left the body, which was carefully mummified to assure the ka a resting place when he needed it. Only through magic protection such as spells, incantation, prayers, and gifts could the ka, having left the dead body, arrive safely at the place of judgment. The ka was a shadowy likeness of the dead body, and swarms of demons and great armies of evil spirits sought to destroy it utterly as it journeyed on its perilous but necessary way to the Great Judgment Hall, where, if it eluded the evil spirits, it stood at last before Osiris and his forty-two lesser gods for judgment. There the ka was required to testify truthfully concerning its earthly life.

The Egyptians pictured this Hall of Judgment, also called the Hall of Two Truths, as a noble place, lofty and austere in the Egyptian manner. Each one of the forty-two lesser gods enthroned beside Osiris was a specialist in some one area of wrongdoing. It was Osiris "the Good Being," "the Lord of Life," the "King of Eternity," who was the ultimate judge of the ka's worth; but as the ka stood before the great throne of Osiris to repeat his detailed "Oath of Clearance," there were those listening to note whether in every small particular he spoke the truth. This is part of the oath, as reproduced in one of its many translations:

> I have not committed fraud and evil against men.
> I have not diverted justice in the judgment hall.
> I have not caused a man to do more than his day's work.
> I have not given away to anxious care.
> I have not been weak.
> I have not been wretched.
> I have not caused a slave to be ill treated by his overseer.
> (Quoted by Atkins, *Procession of the Gods*, 1930, p. 59)

Judgment Day à la Mode

This rather remarkable list is, of course, in addition to disclaimers of the more obvious sins of murder, robbery, sedition, lying, adultery, and to the listing of positively good deeds such as giving food to the hungry and clothes to the naked and ferrying on his way a man who had no boat.

Then lest even Osiris, wise and experienced judge that he is, and his jury of forty-two experts might be mistaken in their judgment, a final infallible test was made of the truth of the Oath of Clearance. The test was infallible because mechanical. The heart of the dead man undergoing trial was placed on one side of the balanced scales of judgment. On the other side Osiris solemnly added the Feather of Truth. If the heart caused the balance to waver, ever so little, a demon stood ready to pounce upon the ka and shred it into tatters. The ka which survived the test passed on to enjoy celestial bliss.

Four thousand years separate Osiris' Hall of Two Truths and the sculptured entrance of Notre Dame Cathedral, but one has only to look up to see there once more the Scales of Truth. There in one scale pan is the dead man's heart, in the other not the feather of truth, but the very demon who should tear the soul to shreds. One longs for the infallible verdict of the feather.

It was far away and long ago, probably the seventh century B.C. and without question in ancient Persia (or Iran) that a remarkable prophet, known to us as Zoroaster, lived. The Persian form of his name was Zarathustra. He proclaimed that there is one God, Ahura-Mazda, the God of light and goodness, to whom is opposed Ahriman, the power of evil and darkness. On the day of Judgment every individual must cross the "Bridge of the Separator" to fall if wicked into the pit of torment, presided over by Ahriman, or proceed if righteous to a paradise called by various names "The House of Song," "The House of Praise" or the "Kingdom of Good Thought," presided over by Ahura Mazda.

In the Persian version of final judgment, as in the Egyptian, the delicate and intricate business of weighing the good against the bad is left to a mechanism, much as we entrust extremely complicated decisions to computers today. Zoroaster's ingeniously sensitive mechanism was the "Bridge of the Separator." It functioned much as an electrically operated garage door does. To drive into his modern garage, the fortunate owner needs only to insert his specially patterned key-card into a slot. Its contact points activate an electric circuit which opens the door. Although unacquainted with garage doors or electricity, Zoroaster anticipated their functions in his bridge.

According to him every human being by his every act throughout his life stamped the pattern of unrighteousness or righteousness into every fiber of his being. At his death, the first impact of his foot upon the Bridge of the Separator, which divided the living from the dead, caused the bridge to respond. If the contact pattern was that of a good man, the bridge widened into a smooth, easy passageway into paradise; if, however, the unfortunate wretch had stamped himself with the pattern of evil, the bridge automatically contracted into a narrowness so razor-sharp the doomed man plunged from the cruel edge into the pit of torment below. It was completely automatic, completely just, and very final.

Zoroaster's account of Doom's Day, the cosmic judgment day, was quite as detailed and graphic as this account of man's personal Judgment Day—and equally stern and relentlessly just. Zoroaster saw the history of human existence as a bitter, unremitting struggle between good and evil. He said that Ahura-Mazda, the wise and good, the spirit of light, supported by his six angels—Good Thought, Right Law, Noble Government, Holy Character, Health, and Immortality—was locked in a death grapple with Ahriman, known also as Angra-Mainyu, the God of Lies, to whose support all the old, discredited gods of the earlier primitive faiths had rushed. Man was free to choose sides, but an onlooker he could not be. All creation, even inanimate nature, was involved decisively on one side or the other, and the involvement was total. No mere bystander's lip service of allegiance counted. Ahura-Mazda demanded hard, grim work from his followers, for the struggle was a grim one and the odds were even. The followers of Ahura-Mazda could be recognized as his not for periodic, ritualistic worship of the Lord of Light, but by the daily, the hourly pattern of their lives. They had to be kind to dumb animals. The penalty for killing a hedgehog, a harmless creature, was

Judgment Day à la Mode

to spend nine life-spans in hell. Industry was piety. "He who sows corn, sows religion," said Zoroaster. To be lazy was to be on the side of evil. "The first man up of a morning will be the first to enter paradise," made clear what sloth was. Fire, although a symbol of Ahura-Mazda, was to be venerated but not worshipped—nor was the disc of the sun Ahura-Mazda, although it shared many of the splendid attributes of that great spirit.

When at the end of time the ceaseless battle beween Ahura-Mazda and Angra-Mainya should come to the final death grapple that Zoroaster called the "Affair," darkness would cover the face of the earth. Fire and the gnashing of teeth in agony, he said, and dreadful wailing will fill the air. The terror clutching all living things on earth will be like the terror of the lamb that is being devoured by a wolf. At the end of the terrible struggle, almost spent, Ahura-Mazda will be victor. At the moment when he struggles to his feet over the prostrate body of his foe, all the hills and all the mountains of the earth will melt into molten lava. Men, both the good and the bad, will have to wade through the rising sea of lava. To the righteous it will feel like warm, soothing milk, and they will move through it easily to safety. At the same time it will sting and sear the wicked and finally scald them to death and utterly destroy them. After Doom's Day will dawn the morning of Paradise on Earth and Ahura-Mazda's Kingdom of Eternal Bliss will begin.

The ancient Greeks believed in a way of reaching justice superior to the mechanical. Three venerable, experienced, and incorruptible men presided over the tribunal in the lower world before which all departed spirits had to appear. There with the leisure of eternity about them in a vast and silent chamber where no wind stirred, the three judges heard and judged the case each soul made for itself. They weighed motives, extenuating circumstances, results, temptations, even as once they had judged living men in Crete. They were the venerable Rhadamanthus, Son of Zeus and Europa and therefore a demigod, and his brother King Minas, famous during his reign in Crete as a just lawmaker, and Acacus, grandfather of the hero Achilles and half brother to Rhadamanthus through their common father, Zeus. No slippery eloquence could deceive them. They looked with steadfast eyes into the minds and hearts of those who came to judgment and were unanimous in verdict. It was like the Greeks to place human standards of justice above a mechanical verdict.

As for the nature of the punishment which awaited evil-doers, Greek tragedy made abundantly clear the nature of nemesis. The Furies with their whips and stings and shrieks brought Judgment Day into the precincts of the human heart. No words more eloquent of human suffering have been penned than those Sophocles and Euripides have used to depict the extreme of human woe when a man stands self-condemned.

For Hindus and Buddhists and their related religionists there was no place in the early formulation of their faiths for the concept of a Judgment Day. Buddha denied there was any meaning to the concept of the soul as substance. You can light one candle from another, he said, but in the second flame have you transferred a substance? Central to the religious teaching of both of these great religions is the idea of law or Karma. This is not law in a legalistic sense, consisting of statutes of divine or human origin that may be followed or disobeyed. It is that far more majestic force, the pattern of being that can be discovered and described but not ordained. And it cannot be broken.

People sometimes speak of "Natural law" as if only relationships between the various aspects of matter were under its domain, but to the Hindu or the Buddhist pondering his probable reincarnation, Karma, the pattern that cannot be broken, the knowledge that what a man now is has already determined what he will be, is all the Judgment Day a man needs.

It is unusual for Western man to envisage life as a wearisome journey and to long for that journey's end in utter quietude or to pray for the wheel of existence to stop turning and pray for the peace that is the peace of absorption into undifferentiated unity. Yet that is the most fervent prayer on the lips of most Hindus and Buddhists. The wish to escape from the painful fragmentation of individual existence into the bliss of eternal oneness of being is so alien to most western religions that it remains for many who hear it formulated a statement on the verbal level, capable of recognition if put into a logically constructed sentence but without reference to any reality.

But when the Hindu personalizes his gods as in the huge three-faced carving in the living rock in the Elephanta Caves near Bombay, the great central face representing Brahma the Creator and the two side faces representing Vishnu the Preserver and Siva the Destroyer respectively, he knows that he is viewing a symbol of the varied aspects of true being, which in its oneness is reality and in its variety illusion, the veil of Maya.

In China, as in India, religious men caught the meaning of Karma, the moving pattern of changeless order. There Lao Tzu built the ethical religion of Taoism upon the declaration that the sum of wisdom and happiness for man was to discover the way the world moves and to move with it. This was to know the Tao. Modern Western men have called it "being in tune with the infinite," "following nature," "accepting the universe." No phrase renders the exact meaning of "Tao," the essence of which is more negative than positive. It is an attitude of surrender, acquiescence, being-at-one-with, or peace. In such a religion Judgment Day is meaningless. What one can say is that there are few or many obstacles separating one from the bliss of absorption in the vastness of eternal being.

Confucianism, while having much in common with Taoism, yet adds its own contribution to the concept of judgment. The bar of judgment before which a man must stand to have his worth tested is the human judgment of his peers. Confucius codified the rules of conduct by which a generation of Chinese judged whether a man might rightly be honored as a "superior man" by the harmony he achieved in his relationships with his fellow men. He was a good man if he played with decorum and integrity the various roles fate decreed for him. Many prefer to call Confucianism an ethical philosophy and no religion, but as it provided countless men for generations with the standards by which they lived, it seems to me to have functioned as a religion.

The Greek philosophy of Stoicism was also venerated as a religion in both ancient Greece and Rome, and because of the doctrine of cyclical destruction and renewal that was so essential a part of it, it contributed to the Christian and Mohammedan doctrine of Doom's Day, at the same time that for a different doctrine also central to it, it read like a variant of Taoism.

Zeno of Cyprus, its founder, was of Phoenician origin and brought with him to Athens doctrines from Semitic Asia. He taught that the Universe was a real being, a living god who had a knowledge of man and desired his good. Periodically, he said, the Universe, which was the body of this living god, was consumed in a cleansing conflagration. From the ashes it renewed itself in the perfect orderly beauty that was its nature. These days of wrath and fiery destruction fitted easily and neatly into the Hebrew and Christian concept of Doom's Day, as it was easy to argue that the fires of the Last Judgment were necessary to wipe out human wickedness and destroy the abominations of mankind. The cleansing fires of the Last Judgment roared through the Universe that from its ashes, Phoenix-like, human life could start afresh.

Thus all eschatology, the doctrine of the last and final things, became increasingly a mixture of doctrines interwoven from many faiths. The cyclical recurrence of a world conflagration, the return of the Golden Age noted in Greek mythology, the Messianic hopes of the Jews, the millenium and the Second Coming of Christ, a shining hope in the New Testament, the New Paradise of Islam—all these concepts, shot through with nature symbols of far earlier religions that signified the succession of seed time and harvest, birth and death, day and night, winter and summer, emerge in areas of the world separated by centuries in time and by seas and mountains and miles in space. The flames of Phaëthon's mythical plunge from high heaven in the chariot of the sun merge in legendary retelling with the flames of Armageddon. There is a central core of agreement under external forms utterly different and complex. As far apart as inscriptions from Mesopotamia in 2000 B.C. and in the prayers of the cargo cults in Melanesia today, we find identical ideas. Thus for centuries a primitive cannibalistic tribe, the Maori of New Zealand, have chanted in their funeral rites a refrain which can be translated:

Judgment Day à la Mode

> Be one with the wide light, the Sun
> With night and darkness, Oh be one, be one.

even as Christians have committed the souls they loved to God from whom they came and the body to the dust from which it was made and to which it returns.

In all the literature having to do with the Day of Judgment, there is nothing in any other sacred book to match the joy with which the Psalmist greeted it in the 96th Psalm. The Hebrews knew that their God, Jehovah, was a just God who never forgot he had created them of fallible dust. Moreover, he was *their* God. They were the people of the Covenant. He was theirs to obey and to honor, but even more, they were his to cherish. In their fealty, lay their complete safety. The closing verses of this psalm of joy have immortalized the concept of final justice. What more is to be sung of its beauty and majesty after this?

> He shall judge the people with equity
> Let the heavens be glad and let the earth rejoice
> Let the sea roar and the fullness thereof
> Let the field exult and all that is therein
> Then shall all the trees of the wood sing for joy
> Before the Lord, for he cometh
> For he cometh to judge the Earth
> He shall judge the world with righteousness
> And the people with his truth.

There is additional cause for joy for Christians because in accordance with the prophecy in Revelations most Christians believe that Judgment Day and the Second Coming of Christ usher in the Millennium, a period of a thousand years of Heaven on Earth. According to Revelations the epoch will begin with the dramatic descent from Heaven of an angel having the Keys of the Abyss and a great chain in his hands. With the chain he will bind Satan, the dragon, the old serpent, and cast him into the abyss and lock it with the great key, and then Satan will remain without power to corrupt Earth for a thousand years or as Daniel would have written "for a time and a time and half a time."

Mohammed, Prophet of Allah, "The One God," "The Merciful," "The Compassionate," made belief in the Day of Judgment one of the important articles of Islamic Faith. There are many Islamic sects today, but all include this belief. It was in Mohammed's hands a patent, because fear-inspiring, weapon against nonbelief. "If," he taught on the Great Day of Judgment, "you are a true believer"—which includes besides belief in Allah and his angels, belief in devils who oppose angels, belief in prophets of whom Mohammed is the greatest, and belief in predestination and the Day of Judgment—then, when you die, you will go to Paradise, a garden of delight with the streams and grassy slopes and the fragrant odors which befit a garden and sweet sounds and pleasant company and delectable food. If you are an unbeliever, then, no matter how righteous your life, you will descend to the graphic tortures of the Seven Terrible Hells.

It is true that followers of Islam can justly claim that their worship of Allah implies a lofty moral code, but also the fact remains that on Judgment Day what tips the balance is not a pure heart against the white feather, but a label, "Believer" or "Nonbeliever."

CHAPTER II

Assorted Angels

As St. Augustine noted in one of his sermons (7, 3), the Greek word *Aggelos*, from which our English word *angel* is derived, indicates an office served rather than a nature. Angels perform the office of intermediaries or messengers between God and Man. This conception seems equally to prevail in primitive as well as in sophisticated religions.

In the Old Testament, the angelic role of mere messenger was expanded into allied roles. Besides being messengers, angels were employed as guards or police officers as, for instance, when they were set to guard the entrance to the Garden of Eden. Sometimes they were given the task of protecting the faithful, as we know from the statement in the 91st Psalm: "For he shall give his angels charge over thee to keep thee in all thy ways." In a very different assignment, they were sometimes ordered to become relentless agents of punishment, every bit as fear-inspiring as the Erinyes or the Eumenides of the Greeks and Romans who filled evil-doers with terror as they fled before them. The 35th Psalm declares: "Let them be as chaff before the wind, and the angel of the Lord driving them on. Let their way be dark and slippery and the angel of the Lord pursuing them."

Angels served also as warriors, and on a memorable day near Jericho, Joshua met and spoke with an angel with a drawn sword who declared himself captain of the "hosts of the Lord." The 103rd Psalm celebrates their loyal obedience and irresistible strength as they stand about the "heavenly throne." "Bless the Lord ye angels of His, ye mighty in strength that fulfill his word." Today we are more apt to think of angels as musicians than as warriors, as harpists and members of choirs. They grace every special heavenly event. Daily and hourly they fill the golden streets of heaven with melodious sound so that it rather than Athens deserves the appellation "City of Song." In Islamic legend, we learn of "the angel, Israfel, whose heart strings are a lute and who has the sweetest voice of all God's creatures."

In Exodus, we are told that Moses ordered goldsmiths to create of beaten gold the images of two cherubim, sheltering wings raised high, to guard the mercy seat above the ark. "Of one piece with the mercy seat shall you make the cherubim on the two ends thereof." Cherubim are a very special form of angel and according to medieval angelology are in the second rank. Medieval scholars, who wrote with authority about angels, divided angels into nine orders, from highest to lowest as follows: seraphim, cherubim, thrones, dominions, virtues, powers, principalities, archangels, angels.

I grant it is a queer list, and one which causes the incredulous to suspect that as a diligent clerk was at work at his high monastic writing desk, a chance gust of wind created havoc. It scattered on the stone floor, with no hint of order, what once perhaps was three neat piles of words. The hapless clerk, unable to reassemble them properly, copied them into the manuscript in the order he had scooped them up from the floor. Once written, that order became the standards which the next clerk obediently followed. I do not say this is what really happened, merely that in spite of much searching I have found no better explanation.

Actually there is a better explanation ready at hand. It is easy to see how the virtues could be personalized and elevated to angelic status, as indeed they are in Zoroastrianism. The letters of Paul to the Ephesians and Colossians offer a further explanation of the "principalities, thrones, dominions and powers". In the second chapter of Ephesians, Paul wrote of Satan as "the prince of the power of the air." And in the following chapter Paul stated his conviction that God had selected him, Paul, though he was "the least of all saints," to reveal God's plan of salvation not only to men but to "the principalities and the powers in the heavenly places." This would seem to indicate his belief that the courts of heaven were indeed royal courts with well-ordered angelic ranks. There is a hint in Paul's letter to the Colossians that he was not in entire sympathy with the angelic pomp of "principalities and powers" and disapproved worshipping high-ranking angels, although the passage is cryptic and easily misread.

In Colossians, when speaking of God's creation of things visible and invisible, Paul gave the list of things invisible as follows: "thrones, or dominions, or principalities or powers." Perhaps Paul was speaking of earthly powers. The angelologists have thought he was definitely speaking of celestial beings. In his epistle to the Romans Paul wrote with defiance and distrust of angels and principalities and powers which might try to come between the faithful and God's love. "For I am persuaded that neither death nor life, nor angels, nor principalities, nor things present nor things to come nor powers, nor height, nor depth, nor any other creature shall be able to separate us from the love of God," he wrote.

And nowhere have I been able to learn of the distinctive appearance of the orders of angels who are "dominions," "powers," "principalities," or "thrones."

The case of seraphim is quite different—the seraphim, or seraphs, are easily recognizable. The head of a seraph has the beautiful perfection of a young child, and when Isaiah saw them in a vision, hovering in adoration above the throne of God, he noted that "above Him stood the Seraphim, each one had six wings: with twain he covered his face, with twain he covered his feet and with twain he did fly." The derivation of their name from a Hebrew root meaning "to burn" accords both with the fervor of their ecstatic adoration of their Lord before whom they chant, "Holy, holy, holy is the Lord of Hosts, the whole Earth is full of his Glory!" and with the brightness of their appearance. When painted, their garments are properly shown as a vivid scarlet. Great poetry, too, recognizes their flame-like nature as in Milton's lines:

> Where the bright seraphim in burning row
> Their loud uplifted angel trumpets blow.

Cherubim, or cherubs, distinguished for the serene certainty of their knowledge, are usually, like seraphim, represented in art with the chubby, innocent faces of children. Sometimes to indicate they are pure intelligence they are represented by the winged heads of children without bodies. However, they may also appear as the full-bodied policemen of heaven, for in Genesis it is recorded that God placed cherubim with flaming swords at the east entrance to the Garden of Eden after Adam and Eve had been driven forth.

Stranger yet, and most uncherubic, as we understand the word today, were the cherubim seen by Ezekiel (Chapters 1-10). With all the careful accuracy of a frightened motorist who has encountered a visitor from Mars, Ezekiel gave both the date and the place of his great encounter with four cherubim. They were driven toward him by a great wind and emerged from a cloud of fiery amber light. They looked like men, but each had four faces and four wings and their feet were shaped like calves' feet. The four faces of each head were, in addition to the usual face of a cherub, a man's face, a lion's, and an eagle's. Ezekiel found it difficult to describe the brightness of their bodies, which were evidently covered with gleaming scales. He said they gleamed like burnished brass or even brighter; they were like burning coals of fire, like torches.

They did not flap their wings but seemed to move stiffly on their sides, as a wheel spins "revolving wheel within wheel," and had additional wheels that seemed self-impelled: "They went everyone straight forward." "And the likeness of the hands of a man was under their wings." It was a terrible vision, which sent Ezekiel forth to foretell the destruction of Israel, saying in the immemorial way of prophets of doom, "Thus saith the Lord."

It is highly probable that many religions have contributed to the conceptions of both seraphim and cherubim. Some authorities connect the name *seraphim* with the Egyptian word *seref*, which means *griffin*. The Britannica states that "the concept apparently derives from ancient near-Eastern folk lore, and the seraphim have been identified with the six-winged figure holding a serpent in each hand portrayed on a relief at Tell Halop, one of the oldest sites in North Mesopotamia."

It is generally agreed, too, that the cherubim got their anatomy

Assorted Angels

in the beginning from Egyptian and Assyrian carved images of winged beasts which guarded royal palaces. In the churches of the twelfth century after Christ, cherubim as winged child-heads, without bodies, were less frequently seen than their representation as a complete child with wings. In the Renaissance and thereafter it became increasingly difficult to be certain that the laughing, dimpled children cavorting on ceilings and panels in baroque exuberance were really cherubim and not Eros, the roguish Greek god of love, or that angels were not Nike, Greek goddess of victory, known to Romans as Victoria.

At the same time archangels became increasingly personalized and humanized even to the extent of being recognizable by their given names. It was of course much earlier, soon after the exile, (cf. Jude 9), that many archangels became known by features as well as duties. Michael, Gabriel, and Raphael were important among the archangels. They were as masculine in appearance as cherubim were predominantly childish. Raphael was one of the seven angels permitted to present the prayers of the saints before the throne. He strode often and confidently into that awful presence. Michael, sword in hand and hair still golden with the flaming radiance of a seraph, did battle with dragons and battled the arch-fiend himself. Lucifer, the arch-fiend, was a fallen archangel described in *Paradise Lost* by Milton in lines which made his name fitting still for the angel who had dropped from the zenith like a falling star.

> His form had not yet lost
> All his original brightness, nor appear'd
> Less than archangel ruin'd, and the excess
> Of Glory obscur'd.

Other archangels had their own particular names and natures, such as Jeremiel, Uriel, Phaltiel, Sandolphin. Some even acquired shrines, as St. Michael did in the fourth century. In Jude it is recorded that Michael struggled with Satan for the corpse of Moses—much as in Persian lore Ormazo, or Mithras, struggled with Ahriman for souls.

Under Byzantine influence, as the Mosaics of Ravenna indicate, angels began to robe themselves in costly and fashionable court dress and when in the early Renaissance female angels first appeared, they eagerly adopted current fashions, usually with an added stole to suggest purity. The growing effeminacy of angels was completed on the Sunday School cards and church calendars of our century. The portrayal of angels went beyond effeminacy; they became smiling, puppet like wraiths, as bloodless as the shades and manes which populated the underworld of Greek and Roman imagination.

In Jewish history one of the distinctions between the Sadducees and the Pharisees was that the former repudiated angels, whereas the Pharisees continued to speak of them, and the Essenes, whose teachings strongly influenced Jesus, believed in them. Jesus himself, according to Matthew (18, 10), suggested the idea of guardian angels for children. Angelic multitudes were witnesses to the significant events of his life from his birth to his ascension. St. Paul's letters to the Thessalonians, the Romans, the Ephesians, and the Colossians, as well as the book of Revelations, show a firm belief in the many offices performed by angels.

The church fathers expended much thought on the subject of angels and brought all their learning to bear on it; although most of us, from all their learned controversy, remember only the hot and absurd debate about how many angels could dance on the point of a needle. To us it is a question to be bracketed with Fuzzy Dog stories. Actually, it arose out of a serious concern with the nature of angels. Were they, as Gregory of Nyssa and Dionysius the Areopagite and Gregory the Great taught, pure intelligences—or did they, as only God was pure spirit, have a body of some kind? Were they created? Probably yes, but when? Was it before the visible world or as part of it? Were they deathless? Or were only some of them deathless? And were others ephemeral as Longfellow indicates in his poem on Sandolphin:

> The Angels of Wind and of Fire
> Chant only one hymn and expire
> With the song's irresistible stress;

Assorted Angels

Expire in their rapture and wonder,
As harp strings are broken asunder
By music they throb to express.

Thomas Aquinas wrote extensively on angels. He put them definitely outside of the material world, for they, he wrote, differ from actual objects in the world of sense. They are not a union of matter and form, which, as Aristotle had demonstrated, is the union necessary for something merely potential to become actual. Angels, Aquinas held, are not to be classified with space-occupying things like tables and chairs. They are unique. They are myriad. They do not "exist," they "are."

Just as in his new book, "The Living God of Nowhere and Nothing," Dr. Nels F. S. Ferre claims that the basic error of intelligent people is to equate reality with substance, so Aquinas had argued that substance must always exist somewhere whereas reality can eternally be, unlimited by time and place, and angels are realities, not beings. They have the reality of Plato's Ideas.

Aquinas held also that angels are free from passions. He said that they never needed to learn because their knowledge is intuitive and immediate and not subject to error. However, the case of Lucifer, who became Satan, contradicts this teaching, for Lucifer had a proud passion for power and he and the other angels who fell with him embraced evil for their good, certainly an horrendous mistake in judgment. Lucifer did not indeed lose all. He is referred to in John as "the Prince of the World," and he was transformed by what was evidently Zoroastrian influence into "The Adversary." Just as in the Persian religion of Zoroastrianism, Angra Manya, Evil incarnate, faced Ahura Mazda, the Good or God, so Satan became the "Adversary" to God in the Hebrew religion.

Angels, as it happened, played most active and important roles in the Zoroastrian religion, which antedated the birth of Christ by some 600 years. Interesting legends involving angels grew up about the infancy of Zoroaster. Zoroaster, when an infant, according to the tale, had been kidnapped by Darasan, a magician, and hidden in a wolf's den. There two angels disguised themselves as nanny goats, entered the den, and suckled the hungry infant. Also, according to legend, Zoroaster came upon his great central religious idea of two cosmic and eternal powers, one good, one evil, from watching the glowing reds and golds and luminous blues of sunset, the garments of angels, fade into the blackness of a starless night. Here he saw Night and Evil, Angra Manya, temporarily overcoming Ahura Mazda and his angels. The names of the six good angels who did the bidding of Ahura Mazda were Good Mind, Good Order, Wisdom, Piety, Well Being, and Immortality.

It would seem obvious from this list that Zoroaster, too, could not have been thinking of angels as "beings," but as "realities." They were not creatures wearing halos, but attributes of the Good. However, for his followers, used to a more primitive religion of many gods, they became beings, celestial presences. Soon his followers knew by name thousands of good angels and feared the 99,999 bad angels, or devils, who lived in hell.

The religion of Islam has much to say of angels, which is not strange as Mohammed, an Arab child born some five hundred and fifty years after the birth of Christ, was well acquainted with the beliefs of Jews and of Christians. As a camel driver in his native city of Mecca, he often listened to their stories of angels as he rested in the market place between trips. Later, when he was twenty-five and his flashing dark beauty and silken beard had captured the heart and hand of the wealthy widow Kadijah, he learned even more about angels from her cousin Warada, who, though an Arab, had been converted to the Jewish faith. He read to Mohammed from the sacred book of the Hebrews.

Thus it happened that as Mohammed, now a merchant prince himself, and a born leader of men, meditated on possible means to reform the dissolute ways of his brother Arabs, he was well prepared to recognize the voice of the angel Gabriel when that angel spoke to him. Gabriel held a golden tablet in his hands as he stood before him and bade Mohammed to read it. Mohammed protested that he had not learned to read, but Gabriel refused to accept such a flimsy excuse, so read the scroll Mohammed did. This was the first of many visits from Gabriel. The Koran is the record of the messages Gabriel brought him directly from Allah.

Assorted Angels

In the Koran, a nobler and more ethical manner of life was dictated to the followers of Islam. The Koran revealed the nature of Allah and of his angels. It taught the meaning of life and death and the hope of immortality. It prescribed the manner of worship, the nature of prayer, and the obligation of pilgrimage.

When Mohammed needed money after his Hegira to Medina, Gabriel gave him valuable advice about waylaying caravans en route to Mecca, which led to successful highway robbery to support an army for Islam.

It was only after Mohammed's death, when he had become "The Prophet," that stories began to circulate about wonderful happenings at the time of his birth. One of the most colorful legends was that at his birth seven thousand angels, disguising themselves as Arabian boys and girls, bathed the baby in a great golden vessel filled with Heavenly Dew.

An orthodox Moslem, no less than a Christian, is taught to believe in a hierarchy of angels. They are sexless beings, although they may bear men's names. They have no need for food or drink, and their sole wish is to praise Allah, carry out his wishes and do his bidding. Israfel, the angel with the sweet voice, whom I have already mentioned, is the angel designated to sound the trumpet to awaken the dead on Judgment Day, and Azrail is the Angel of Death. Malik rules over Hell and is almost an exact opposite of Mikail, the bright Angel of Heaven.

The followers of Islam believe that every human being has not one but two attending angels, serving not so much as guardians, but as recording angels, to note his slightest deviation from righteousness. In addition, two more angels visit a person in his tomb to examine him *viva voce*, and if he fails to pass this final examination that shows whether or not he has kept the faith, they flog him unmercifully.

It should be noted, in passing, that some Christians believe that every person has two attendant angels and that one is a man's good angel who tries to keep him from harm and temptations to wrongdoing and the other is a bad angel, a very devil, trying to lead him astray. This is very likely an inheritance from Persia and the Zoroastrian theme of the eternal struggle of good and evil. It is not a comfortable or a prideful doctrine, as it reduces man to pretty much of a puppet on a string.

It is difficult to distinguish between angels, good and bad, and the good and evil spirits whom one finds not only in Islamic legends but in the legends that grow up under the shelter of almost all religions. They antedate Queen Scheherazade and the Arabian Nights. The genii and Ifrits, slaves of lamp and ring, as well as the devils, demons, nixies, prixies, gnomes, goblins, and vampires, flourish in Taoism as well as in sheltering Christian and Buddhist superstition. They may well be the descendants of the nature spirits worshipped in the animistic stage of primitive religions. They had their counterparts in Greek and Roman mythology. Some of them are graceful beings dancing through our fancy still as nymphs or as dryads, those very special nymphs who are the shy souls of trees. To admit them to the company of angels would cause confusion. They are essentially earthbound creatures, although now and then they may have mingled with heavenly visitants undetected.

They were not angels any more than the Greek and Roman heroes were, who, after death reached the Isles of the Blessed. The pale shades drifting like dried leaves in the dour regions beyond the Styx were in no sense angelic. Our ancient Norse ancestors believed that heroes dying in battle were transported bodily to Valhalla by the awful and beautiful maidens of Odin, the Valkyries, who were angels. The warriors, however, whom the Valkyries carried to their unending banquet remained warriors capable of endless delight in food and drink, for which a proper angel never has need or appetite.

Certain revolutionary religious sects, notably the Mormons or Latter-Day Saints, have utterly revised the ancient ideas of angels and humanized them completely. Gone are the scales, the wings, the calves' feet, the blazing hair. The Mormons hold that angels are resurrected human beings, fashioned like living men in the image of God, not creatures of flight, not birds. Thus the angel Moroni, a slender golden sentinel atop one of the spires of the Mormon Temple in Salt Lake City, holds a long trumpet raised toward the encircling mountains. He is wingless, but in command of space. He is a very human angel.

Implicit in the widespread hope of immortality is this doctrine, made explicit by the Mormons, that the angelic state of being is the human state perfected. Few of us would honestly wish to be assured of an eternity of existence as a being by definition as non-human as an orthodox angel. What we want is to continue to be ourselves, our very human selves, our ideal selves to be sure, forever at our best. We ignore the fact that a person is an event, forever changing. We freeze the continuity we feel as self into an imagined eternity of sameness.

Crippling age must drop away, but our maturity remain. Problems must disappear, but our strength and wisdom to solve them remain. The heavenly mansions we shall inhabit may be close to places where traditional angels dwell. Their wings may beat the air about us in steady flight; their music fill our ears, but closer to us will be our friends and loved ones, not strange and sexless creatures. The mother, the father, the husband, the child we once mourned, we shall find again even as we find them in memory, unchanged and precious.

Most convincing proof of the tendency to think of the dead as living on as angels with special tasks to do is found throughout Christendom beginning toward the close of the fourth century. It became customary to place the various parts of the body, which had been under the influence of the signs of the Zodiac when astrology was in the ascendant, under the particular care of special saints. Thus one made a prayer to St. Blasius, if one had a sore throat or congested lungs. St. Erasmus was kept busy with ills of the abdomen, and two saints, Lucia and Triduana, watched over the eyes. St. Vitus could heal choreas, as we become aware from the term "St. Vitus Dance." One prayed to St. Anthony to ease the burning fire of erysipelas, and as late as the fifteenth century St. Roch was asked to work overtime when the dread plague struck. Then, there are kindly saints who help one find misplaced articles. Indeed, saints "who from their labors rest" would seem to have no leisure at all as angels in heaven.

Wordsworth, restating our age-old belief, suggested that birth is but "a sleep and a forgetting" and life a brief lapse from eternity into time. If so, we have forgotten, too, that individuality is bound up with time and finite space. It is the product of limitation, and as followers of Hinduism rightly say, Eternity and Infinity are incompatible with it. Angels must remain traditional; human angels are illogical. Moreover, our space age has left no living space for traditional angels. As jets skim over the billowing cloud floors of high heaven, they find no ladders with angelic throngs reaching from the cloud floor through blue air tunnels to a lonely Jacob slumbering in the desert. No archangel ever intercepts a guided missile on its calculated path. No astronaut, though he should walk in space around the world, would ever encounter an angel there. Nor is there need for messages written in golden words on angels' scrolls. By microscope and by telescope, by infrared light and ultra violet, by X rays and by hard labor, men of science have become the messengers to reveal the ways of God to man. They and they alone perform that most compassionate of the angelic tasks: they gather up men's worthy prayers for health, and a better, freer, nobler life and lift them toward fulfillment.

CHAPTER III

"Turn but a Stone, and Start a Wing"

Parents are often impatient with the ceaseless "Why" of their children. However, the ability to ask "Why" is one of the child's most valuable assets, even as it was invaluable for primitive man eons ago in his cave. It shielded him from danger quite as much as his strong club and the stones he learned to hurl. An impatient parent often gives his child a carelessly incomprehensible answer to his legitimate question, and even so primitive man often had an incomprehensible answer to his question.

Why did the stone, on which he had stepped so often, start this time to roll so that he fell painfully on the slope? The only voice to answer primitive man was his own, from within him. It suggested the stone was wearied of being stepped on. It willed to roll; the wrong answer, but an answer; and it was corroborated, so it seemed, by other events. When hail-stones beat upon him, they wanted to hurt him. As he emerged from the chill of his cave and sat on a log, the warm sun patted his back and he felt its hands upon him with kindly intent. Thus the peopling of his world with spirits went on. Whenever he achieved an explanation, he held to it tenaciously, for the most frustrating experience for any human being is to have "Whys" unanswered. So the cave man held fast to his animistic wrong answer and taught it to his children. Naturally, when a great shadow began to devour the midday sun, they remembered the magic their father had taught them and, like him, by creating a great din were able to frighten away an evil-minded spirit. A surmise became a tradition.

The faith of primitive man was of necessity a stubborn thing. For him to survive, it had to be as stubborn as his will, as strong as his club. It was the armor he had made for himself, naked as he was, or the armor he inherited from his father. He kept on forging it anew, but in the pattern he knew, so that he and his group could deal with an often hostile environment.

Primitive man's animistic explanation of the things that befell him as the result of the good or evil intention of what we call the inanimate world, false though it was, benefited him in the end. It suggested a plan of action, and it thereby released him from the paralyzing inaction of total fear.

His animistic explanation was false, but he believed in it and was comforted. Even a false feeling of security is a precious relief while it lasts, and sometimes it lasts a long time. Certain false beliefs have been known to give men peace and comfort all their lives and to have glowed before their dying eyes with the full luster of truth.

Primitive man, being forced to observe in order to survive, increasingly perfected his ability to connect cause and effect, the pragmatic wisdom we call "common sense." It was an uncritical bundle of knowledge. A total situation with irrelevant items was just as often connected in its entirety with a resulting event as was the single relevant item with its inevitable sequence. Common-sense beliefs were sense compounded with nonsense.

That was one aspect of primitive man's thinking; another was that he could not transcend his experience any more than we can. He could only rearrange it. Moreover, his experience was narrow to a degree difficult for us to comprehend. As a human being, he was aware of his own fears and his own desires and not unnaturally ascribed them, even as a child does today, equally to a hailstone that pelted and wounded him and to a wild beast that clawed and bit him.

Scientists agree that primitive thinking is universally and inevitably animistic. We, today, often naïvely assume that others feel as we do about some vexing problem. The primitive man merely universalized our uncritical thinking. He found "spirit" in everything, and most spirits were hostile. When life is lived at its lowest potential, it is indeed the nasty, brutish, short life described by Hobbes. It seemed natural to primitive man that violence and death should lurk for him at every turn. His main

"Turn but a Stone, and Start a Wing"

concern was to thwart and outwit and destroy evil spirits.

Animism is properly defined as a collection of more or less closely related beliefs. It is animistic to believe that all natural objects, trees, rivers, mountains, not excluding the universe itself, have "souls." Even if one hesitates to believe in so elevated a thing as a soul, it is still animistic to believe they have impersonal "mana" or will-power. It is still animistic to believe that souls may exist apart from their material bodies. Animism explains death, and its brother, sleep, as the permanent or temporary absence of the soul from its natural body. Madness is often explained as the possession of a body by an alien soul, often an evil one, a very devil. Our speech reflects this today. "I don't know what possessed you!" says a mother shaking her naughty but precious child, or we excuse ourselves for stupidity or dereliction saying: "I don't know what possessed me to say or do that."

The inevitable conclusion to the animistic premise is belief in a countless multitude of spirits deceiving and confounding men at every step as adroitly and expertly as ever Ariel misled the shipwrecked crew at Prospero's command. This legion of spirits has many names. They are elves, dwarfs, goblins, ghosts, fairies, fays, prexies, leprechauns, nixies, sprites, brownies or, from classical culture, genii. The pair of genii, a good genius and an evil genius, assigned at birth to pilot a person throughout his life and becoming in the New Testament guardian angels, are of more than passing interest.

Even as a person's genius may be good or bad, so the many spirits that inhabit the world are both beneficient and malign. There is little in common, except their supernatural natures, between the fairy godmothers who protect the Cinderellas of the world and ugly leprechauns bent on mischief. Pookas and knockers and bogles are malice personified. They may have originated in the imaginings of cave men when evils aplenty lurked in the shadows of the dank dens they called home.

The dreadful "golems" of Hebrew legend are quite another and very sophisticated matter. They are automata in human form, of human manufacture, equipped with life by human agency, and precursors of the monsters of science-fiction that haunt our television screens today. Under the disguise of their mechanistic structure, they owe their goblin horror, as do their modern counterparts, to the old animistic assumption that disembodied mind can exist independently and can be joined to inert matter.

According to Mohammedan mythology, Jinns or jenni are a class of spirits, lower than the angels. They are really demons, valuable as servants, if one knows how to control them by lamp or ring or incantation, but potentially destructive.

The manner of thinking that resulted in animistic beliefs did far more than people the earth with spirits of light and darkness. It determined the nature of the high gods themselves. Again and again, in country after country man created his gods in his own image. He endowed his gods with his own love of circumstance and power. They needed and enjoyed food and drink. They loved and hated. They were male and female. Many of the spirits, born of animistic beliefs, spirits of heavenly bodies or mountains, or rivers, became gods in their own right. In this fashion Jahweh, God of the Mountain, became Jehovah.

We tend to think of animism as exclusively primitive religious thinking and consequently fail to recognize it when we encounter it in contemporary religious belief. A religious group, the Shakers, originating in England and emigrating to America, offer an interesting example of the survival of animistic thinking. They fled from England in 1774 and prospered in North America where they once had a membership of over six thousand. Now they have dwindled to a membership of some twenty or fewer "Old Women." Their founder, "Mother Ann Lee," taught that God is both male and female. His masculine nature was manifested in Jesus, and in 1736 his femininity was incarnated in a girl child Ann, born to a blacksmith and his wife in Manchester, England. She became a textile worker, illiterate, but with a majestic dignity which commanded instant respect. A biographer described her as short, rather stout, blue-eyed, chestnut-haired, and commanding. However, no matter how commanding or how gracious the human body in which an alien spirit takes up its abode, it is animistic thinking to believe it possible. Salem witches afforded another all too recent and pitifully tragic instance of animism.

"Turn but a Stone, and Start a Wing"

Idols are in a somewhat different category from an animated automation such as a golem. The spirit that inhabits the idol does so independently of human contriving. The teraphim spoken of in the Old Testament in connection with the early history of the Jewish people were idols. Details as to their configuration indicate they were probably of human shape and undoubtedly usually less than life size. Otherwise, Rachel could not have hidden the family teraphim in the camel's gear or sat upon them when her father, Leban the Syrian, searched her tent. The whole story of her theft of the household gods and the clever ruse she used to insist upon remaining seated on the camel's furniture reads like an ancient gossip column. No less exciting as a news story is the account in First Samuel of using the teraphim as a dummy in David's bed to enable David to escape when mad and wrathful Saul sought to slay him.

In Genesis, the teraphim are mentioned in the conclusion of a horror story of mass murder, perpetuated by Jacob's sons to avenge the rape of their sister Dinah. Their father, after the murder, certain of retribution from the Canaanites and the Perizzites, prepared to flee to Bethel with all his wives and children, servants, and flocks. His orders preparatory to departure were: "Put away the strange gods that are among you and purify yourselves and change your garments." Evidently Rachel's teraphim had multiplied. We learn of their banishment again at a later time. In Second Samuel there is an account of King Josiah's cleansing of his kingdom. We learn: "Moreover them that had familiar spirits, and the wizards, and the teraphim and the idols and the abominations that were espied in the land of Judah and in Jerusalem did Josiah put away."

It is evident from the context in Ezekiel and in Zechariah and Hosea that the teraphim, along with the ephod, were used in divination rites. As late as the eighth century B.C., they were employed to fortell national safety and in earlier monarchical days had their place on household altars as well.

As one reads of the teraphim, one thinks inevitably of the Roman *lares* and *penates* with which we are more familiar, possibly because their names have not been classified with abominations but have passed into our common speech as a synonym of home.

The Lar, used most often in the plural Lares, was from immemorial time in Italy a guardian god of cross-roads. Then the Lares quite literally moved in out of the cold and went and took places warmed by the hearth in the inner room, the *atrium* of Roman homes, there to become tutelary gods.

Thanks to an ancient bronze statue of a Lar in the Museo dei Conservatori in Rome, we have knowledge of their appearance. The Lar in Rome had a youthful, boyish figure and wore a short, high-girt tunic that became him. He held a saucerlike cup in one hand and a drinking horn in the other. The whole figure was animated. The smile of the round-cheeked youth reminds one of Donatello's "Laughing Boy." This bronze image is thought to have been a *lar familias* or protector of the family which, in case the family moved, would be taken with it and set up again in a niche of honor in the new home.

There were twenty or more types of Lares, which differed in appearance. Some were carved from wood, some were sculptured in stone or marble, and others were bronze. They were less than life size. Some Lares continued outdoor police duty, for the *lares semitales* protected footpaths and by-ways. Would that they had not forsaken their task! *Lares praestites* protected the state in general. Others watched over farmers, herdsmen, soldiers, sailors, and travellers. In fact, there was a helpful, kindly Lar for almost every hazard of life and almost every calling.

Grateful people saw to it that the Lares received their due reward. It was to them each morning the *pater familias* offered a prayer. Before them at each meal, a member of the family placed an offering of food. On festive days, such as birthday celebrations, besides receiving a food offering of roast pork, wine, cakes, and honey, they were garlanded with flowers. They fared very well housed in their niche, one on either side of an image of Vesta, goddess of the hearth, or more likely still, on either side of the family genius. The genius was an Apollo-like youth engaged in sacrifice.

A word must be said about the genius, literally "the begetter."

He was a symbol of family continuity, the continuance of the *gens*, the sacred power inherent in the father and mother of the family to continue the line. Later the genius lost its early meaning and was confused with the Greek *daimon*, the guardian spirit, or even with the "higher self" of each member of the group. In 8 B.C., Horace, the Roman poet, described the genius as "a god who is born and dies with each one of us," which easily yields to our contemporary use of the word though with additional meaning.

The presence of these household gods, or at least their sacred images in the atrium, the very center of the family dwelling, helps to explain the admirable Roman feeling about the sacredness of home. The home was also a temple, and from this the idea of family acquired a proud stability and the dignity of enduring things.

The state Lares were represented on old Roman coins as youths in semimilitary dress with lances. On the coins they were represented as seated with a dog, symbol of watchfulness, lying at their feet.

We usually speak of the lares and penates together as household gods. The *penates di* were gods of the store room, *the penetralia*. Even the high gods, Jupiter, Juno, Venus, and their peers, were sometimes called penates. From earliest antiquity into the fifth century A.D., there are references to penates and their offices, although they are not always clearly distinguished from lares. On coins they often appear as twins like Castor and Pollux. On the Sacred Way near the Palatine in Rome, there was a temple to Romulus and Remus, founders of Rome; but as guardians of Rome, it is not clear whether they were lares or penates, for the hearth and table were as sacred to the penates as to the lares. Together they meant home.

With the decline of the Roman Empire, these friendly spirits that guarded homes also passed away, but not into complete oblivion. Their counterparts are still honored in certain Oriental homes today.

A visitor to Bangkok, Thailand, may find in many Buddhist homes in a corner of the best room in the house, whether it is a living room or an elegantly appointed drawing room, an image of the Buddha. It may be a statue resplendent in gold leaf and seated on a lotus blossom throne or a delicate tiled mosiac built into the wall. Also, by the entrance door or attached to the compound gate he will probably see a shrine no larger than a small bird cage, housing the miniature household gods. If located by the compound gate, the shrine may be dusty from the traffic of the street, along which at dawn saffron-clad monks come with their enormous begging bowls. In a humbler home, enclosed only on three sides, it may be stained with spray from traffic from the Klong beside which the household lives. Tiny as the shrine is, and shabby as it may be, it will have its offering of flowers. The favor of the household gods is still invoked, albeit with a gesture that is careless or half-in-jest. The flowers are likely to be not merely faded but actually dried with neglect, and seldom, if ever, I surmise, do these tiny gods know the savor of fresh roast pork or the sweet fragrance of wine.

In Japan, the tutelary gods have in many places left the snug interiors of the homes they guard to perch upon the gable-ends of the roof-tree, in the shape of dragons. They are dog-like dragons who, as they crouch, resemble still the faithful watchdogs of the Roman coins. One with a glaring dragon-face forms his lips to blow away all evil influences such as spirits of illness and misfortune, while his mate with open jaws breathes in all the beneficent spirits of the air. They guard temples as well as homes.

We have not outgrown the need for the protective services of household gods and could use a few dragon-dogs on the roof-trees of our Western homes. Perhaps if they perched there above us, blowing away evil influences and breathing in good spirits, our homes would become once more abiding places, rather than points of departure. "Homesickness" has a strangely opposite meaning in our century than in centuries preceding ours. Too often the children of our homes pine, not to return home, but to escape from it. They are sick *of* it, not *for* it. They want their own apartments, or even less, a transient corner in a room crowded with others of their age who are also escaping. Perhaps dragon-dogs, or lares, or genii, could bring these wandering children back to the homes from which they are so often, but certainly not always, sorely missed.

One can purchase in Japan small ceramic replicas of the guardian dragon-dogs, which are properly not dogs at all but highly conventionalized lions. They are called *Kara shi shi*, or temple lions. One expects to find them protecting palace doorways, the approaches to temples and shrines, entrances to tombs—in short, anything sacred or holy. Their presence at the gable-ends of the roof-tree of a home puts it under celestial care. They may be distantly related to the seraphim.

They or their sculptured predecessors have been guardians for centuries. The almost vestigial wings on the hind legs of the modern ceramic model, easily overlooked or mistaken for a ruff of dragon-hair, proclaim their relationship to winged feline sculpture from Assyria centuries before Christ. There, too, winged lions stood guard. They made their way, sanctioned by animistic belief, from Assyria to Iran, from Iran to India and China, and from China to Japan. They were modified as they moved, but steadfast in their guardian role.

Even as a shi-shi from modern Japan can still be purchased to link us with the second or third century B.C. in Assyria, so animism, man's oldest religion, can still be found active today. If you fail to identify it, look for vestigial wings, for like Japanese shi-shi, it has them.

There is no need, however, to travel as far from home as Japan or Thailand to find the fruit of animistic assumption in contemporary religion. All thinking in which is implicit the generalization that the soul inhabits the body as an owner inhabits his house is animistic; when we speak of the soul leaving the body at death we are speaking animistically. Not so many years ago it was common to think of certain illnesses, notably epilepsy, as cases of possession, in which an evil spirit was contesting with the person's true self, or soul, for possession and control of the body.

Of the books of the New Testament the Gospel according to Luke expounds this doctrine most clearly. Luke's account of the madman who was possessed of devils, which Jesus cast out and which entered a herd of swine that thereupon plunged down a steep hillside to their death in the lake below, is told as a simple straightforward tale of an event needing no explanation. The amazing aspect of Luke's account of the countless miracles of healing and even the resurrection of those already dead is Luke's matter-of-fact relating of each event. The explanation of each miracle is simple and matter-of-course if one accepts his animistic generalization about indwelling spirits good and bad, which recognize the authority of a superior spirit of supreme purity and power. There is no need for even an exclamation point in the telling. Luke, the physician, quite as genuinely as any shaman in a primitive tribe, believed in demoniac possession. Sometimes the primitive healer, as we know from the study of ancient skulls, resorted to trepanning the skull of the possessed (i.e., sick) person to allow the evil spirit to escape. Hideous noise, nauseous smells or tastes, or beatings sometimes frightened the demon and caused it to leave the affected one.

Luke, more sophisticated and humane than a primitive shaman, was confident that supreme goodness could by its presence conquer evil. This is faith-healing at the highest point of animistic thinking. This Gospel of St. Luke has in all probability done more to strengthen the various Christian sects in whose creeds healing by faith is an essential tenet than any other part of the Bible. There is another kind of faith-healing, not to be confused with it, which is an aspect of psychosomatic teaching. It is sometimes spoken of as "positive thinking" and is that stubborn, resolute, valiant part of courage that refuses to cry quits. To be distinguished from both of these, there are still, for suggestible people suffering from conversion hysteria, miracle-shrines all over the world piled high with crutches and canes, left by people once paralyzed who now walk, or once blind who now see, but their stories belong more properly to a discussion of psychology than religion.

CHAPTER IV

The Food Mystique

Most of us are, fortunately, close enough to primitive ways of thinking to accord "a willing suspension of disbelief" to Lewis Carroll's food magic. We are not like Alice, who protested to the Queen that she couldn't believe *impossible* things, but far more like the Queen who retorted to Alice that she dared say Alice hadn't had much practice and that sometimes she, the Queen, had believed as many as six impossible things before breakfast. In Wonderland Alice had plenty of practice in accepting the impossible. She nibbled a cake and grew to enormous size in a twinkling; nibbled another and shrank to a perilous miniature of herself. She learned that food could have powers other than those of nutriment. For noncritical, primitive thinking this is merely an obvious truth. If a hunter eats the heart of a lion, he too, becomes lion-hearted. He has partaken of the courage and strength of his prey, as well as his flesh. If a cannibal, after killing a crafty enemy, eats his brains, he will possess his enemy's wiles as well as his flesh.

On the face of it, a report from a reputable experimental psychologist quoted by Steven M. Spencer in an article in the *Saturday Evening Post* of September 24, 1966, might seem scientific confirmation of this ancient superstition. The psychologist, Dr. James McConnell, working in a mental health research laboratory in Michigan, found that if he sacrificed the flat-worms that he had carefully trained in goal-seeking as a meal for untrained flat-worms, the meal served the banqueting flat-worms not merely as nourishment but as education. The skill the sacrificial flat-worms had acquired by training was passed on to the flat-worms who ate them. Statistics showed that after dining on the educated flat-worms they made significantly fewer errors in reaching their goal in a maze than other flat-worms who had not dined on such superior food. The explanation for the miraculous transference of memory was, however, the reverse of primitive thinking, which involves the thesis that bits and scraps of thought material are swallowed along with goblets of fat and sinew. Only an advanced biochemist could fully understand the explanation, involving as it does RNA and DNA molecules. I admit it still looks like magic to me.

Those of us who are often called "the people of the Book" are familiar with the mysterious properties of the fruit of two fair and forbidden trees that grew in the Garden of Eden. Adam and Eve ate of the fruit of the first tree, probably an apple, and like the flat-worms in so doing acquired the knowledge of good and evil. The knowledge which the flat-worms acquired by eating their trained relatives was which way to turn to avoid punishment and to acquire food. That obviously was also knowledge of good and evil.

The knowledge of the values of good and evil that Adam and Eve learned was, as we their descendants know, infinitely more complex, leading to sorrow and hard labor. Adam and Eve were driven out of their idyllic garden before they had opportunity to eat the fruit of the second tree. Had they eaten it, they would have become immortal. What they learned, to their sorrow, from the apple they ate was that there is a difference between good and evil, but they did not eat enough to learn exactly what that difference is and so were less fortunate than the flat-worms, who were able to learn the invariably correct response between alternate courses.

There is in the Malay language a saying used as highest praise It is "Awak suda makan garam," which can be translated, "You have tasted salt." To say this to a person is to praise not so much his learning as his wisdom. It is a tribute to his ability to discriminate and judge, almost as if the salt gave him a power to see beneath the surface of facts. As sometimes happens in a metaphor, the simple statement goes beyond the simile that could state only that just as tasting salt heightens awareness of true taste qualities, so what you have experienced has heightened your power to savor

The Food Mystique

life fully. The Malay compliment implies a permanent faculty, added not by experience, but by salt.

A Gaelic legend which accounts for the formation of the River Boyne is an interesting variation of the Hebrew myth of the tree of the knowledge of Good and Evil. Formerly, at what is now the source of the Boyne, there was a well, cool and deep, in the shade of nine hazel trees. These magic trees bore crimson hazelnuts, which like the apples of Eden had the power of bestowing omniscience upon anyone who ate them. But, according to the legend, the privilege of eating the nuts was reserved for several great salmon who lived in the well and after the manner of fish did not divulge what they alone knew. The gods themselves were forbidden access to the well. One of the goddesses, Boam, wife of Daga, "the good god," was as curious as Eve. She approached the well, intent on securing and eating a hazel-nut. At her approach, the waters of the well rose up out of their deep pit and forming a torrent, swept her with them far from the trees. Being a goddess, she escaped with her life, but the faithful guardian waters continued to flow and do so to this day. In the depths of the waters of the River Boyne, the salmon still swim, looking in vain for the marvelous nuts they once ate when they were known as "the salmons of knowledge."

Throughout history as recorded in legends, the many different gods men have worshipped have evidently been in agreement about keeping for themselves any food that bestows immortality. The nectar and ambrosia which graced the table of the Olympians was carefully denied to their worshippers, lest they, partaking of this fragrant fare, should like the gods become immortal. The Greek gods enjoyed other food as well, sent to them from sacrificial altars, on savory waves of odors of roasting beef or lamb. That gave them pleasure for the moment, but the nectar and ambrosia kept them forever young, beyond all touch of time.

The goddess Demeter, it is true, in the barren year of her self-exile from Olympus, while grieving for her lost daughter Persephone, purposed to give immortality and perpetual youth to a mortal child. The child's parents, Metaneira and Celeus, had taken pity on her as a bedraggled old woman seeking a lost child. As such, they invited her to share the poor cottage where they lived with no suspicion they were entertaining a goddess.

One night, Metaneira, sleeping lightly to be alert to her baby's slightest cry, saw the strange old woman steal to his cradle and then, holding the child in her lap, anoint him from head to feet with a fragrant oil. She could not know that the fragrance which filled the cottage was from ambrosia, which when rubbed upon the child's body protected it forever from bodily harm—no knife could cut, no fire could sear his flesh thereafter. When the frightened mother saw the old crone about to lay the child on the red embers of the hearth to complete the spell which would have made the baby immortal, she snatched the child from her, and drove Demeter forth. The tale has several morals that have doubtless been voiced repeatedly down the centuries. It also reaffirms the belief in powers beyond the merely nutritional in food.

The secret and sometimes terrible power of food is manifested in a later chapter of this same story of Demeter, the earth-goddess, and her daughter Persephone, stolen from her by Hades, King of the Dead, ruler of the underworld. Demeter's grief for her lost daughter and consequent long neglect of the fields and the resultant famine on earth induced Zeus himself to send Hermes, messenger of the gods, to stand before the throne of Hades in the underworld and plead for the release of Hades' pale, reluctant bride, stolen from the flowery fields of earth. As Hermes stood before Hades with the demand from Zeus that Persephone must be permitted to return to the upper world of earth, made barren by her mourning mother's neglect, Hades persuaded his bride to taste one single pomegranate seed for his sake. He knew, though Persephone did not, that if even one seed passed her fasting lips she would be bound to return to him, as indeed she does for four months of chill winter. And when, as spring, Persephone returns to earth, she is no longer the simple, laughter-loving, flower-bedecked maiden she once was, but brings with her some of the chill grayness of the world of the dead, where for four months each year she is enthroned as Queen.

In that world of the dead are mighty rivers. The water of one

The Food Mystique

of them, Lethe, River of Forgetfulness, has strange powers. Anyone drinking that water loses all memory of his past. On its banks crowd the souls of all who are fated to live again in the world above. As Anchises told his son Aeneas, who while still living braved the descent beside foul Lake Avernus to visit him, a goblet of water from Lethe is "a long drink of oblivion."

Men at other times in other places have believed that more than forgetfulness can be imbibed. Our Norse ancestors believed that wisdom could be quaffed from a cup, but always for a price. Their gods, unlike the Greek gods, were not immortal. They were always aware of their impending twilight and doom. Nor were they omniscient like the Hebrew god, but they were for the most part noble and heroic. Odin, who like Zeus was the sky-father, was most noble, most heroic, and most benevolent. "Clad in a cloud-fray kirtle and a hood as blue as the sky," he sought more knowledge to postpone as long as possible the inevitable twilight of the gods and that final day of doom for men and gods alike, "Ragnarok." In the legends we are told of the brooding Odin who sat apart, eating no food at feasts in his palace Gladscheim or in Valhalla at the banquets of victorious warriors. But he willingly paid with the loss of one eye for a deep draught from the Well of Wisdom. With this dearly bought knowledge, he protected both the gods and men for many long years. He even risked his life to wrest from the giants and give to gods and men the mead that made anyone tasting it a poet.

Turning back again from the chill gray North to Homer's wine-bright seas and Odysseus, sailing from Troy on the long, perilous voyage home to Ithaca, we are told that Odysseus came after ten days to the land of the "Lotus Eaters." There his crewmen ate "honey-sweet buds" of lotus with the effect, Tennyson says, that to each of them "It seemed always afternoon." Whether, as Homer implies, this was a magic effect or, as we in our chemistry-conscious age would surmise, a chemical intoxication from an hallucinatory drug, one is free to choose. The men were so filled with the lazy enjoyment of the sensuous present that they lost ambition, had no care for the future, ceased to think of their distant homes, and had to be bound by ropes to their places at the oars.

There was no doubt about Circe's acorns. They worked their transformation by sheer magic. It was the enchantresses' magic that changed the crewmen who ate her acorns into swine. The crewmen appeared like swine in the sty in which Circe penned them, but they had the sensibilities of men and loathed the vile sty and themselves as only men with all their understanding and emotions could loathe. Only Homer's imagination and the possible need to point a moral could have given acorns such power.

Before chemistry became a science, it was easy, perhaps inevitable, to ascribe to magic the properties of foods and drinks we now explain in terms of chemical reactions with accompanying physiological and psychological results. For example, in Mexico, even before the Aztecs, a mushroom called *Leonancil* or the Divine Mushroom, was eaten under the supervision of a high priest in a religious ceremony to produce mind-expanding visions. The ceremony was known as "eating God's flesh," and the vision was no doubt comparable to an LSD trip. In the dimness of time, long before the Christian era, recorded in Sumerian, the oldest-known written language, there is evidence of a religious cult that worshipped what was probably the same sacred mushroom, *amanita muscario*, as the flesh of a god. When eaten the mushroom acted as a powerful hallucinatory drug. Obviously its use had to be controlled. How better than by religious ritual?

Similarly *Soma*, the sacred drink praised in the Rig Veda of early Hindu worship, was undoubtedly a psychedelic, as it was made from a plant, perhaps hemp, during the course of the sacrifice. The herb was pressed between stones, mixed with milk, strained, and drunk at once, allowing no time for the production of alcohol. Its effects, as described in a surviving hymn to Soma, were vivid hallucinations accompanied by the illusion of expanding to enormous size. So important was Soma to the ancient Hindus that it soon acquired its own divinity, the god Soma.

Zoroastrians in Persia had a similar drink that they called

The Food Mystique

haoma, which is merely the Iranian equivalent of the Hindu word Soma. Strangely enough, even today when chemical knowledge is widespread, a segment of young Americans regard psychedelics as avenues for religious, or at least mystic experience instead of tools of chemical destruction.

A curious dilemma in regard to the enforcement of certain food and drug laws confronts officials in the national capital today. It has to do with the use of the peyote bud in solemn religious ceremonies by certain Indian tribes, notably those along the Rio Grande. Teachers on the reservations have noted that bright-eyed, eager Indian boys and girls, who may have made rapid progress in the lower grades, all too often become listless high school dropouts. It may be highly significant that at this age they begin to participate as adults in the formal worship of their god, which includes ingesting the body of their god in the form of peyote buds in solemn communion rites. It is a common complaint about mature Indians that they are too often content to drift; they lack ambition; they will live in squalor rather than exert themselves. Homer recorded the syndrome in Odysseus' crewmen. The lotus flowers of Homer and the dried cactus fruit called peyote would seem both to possess a mind-expanding chemical. The Greeks considered the power magical; the Indians consider it religious.

The Indian, of course, has his own doctrine of the transubstantiation of the cactus bud into the body of his God, well aware that it parallels the doctrine the missionaries have tried to teach him of the change of the bread and wine in the Eucharist into the blood and flesh of the crucified Saviour.

In a column of "The National Observer" for January 15, 1968, an interesting report signed by reporter Steward Davis from Austin, Texas, tells of the plight of the many Indians who belong to the "Native American Church of North America". Indians of several tribes outside of Texas, notably some Cheyenne and Navajo, Omaha and Winnebago Indians, belong to this church.

A Texas law went into effect August 28, 1967, that made the sale or use of the mind-expanding dried cactus fruit, peyote, illegal. Roughly 200,000 members of this flourishing church, from the Rio Grande to the pine woods of Wisconsin, have been using peyote regularly. They eat the dried cactus bud, about the size of a silver dollar, in order to "absorb God's spirit" or in other words have an experience similar to an LSD trip. They compare taking the peyote to taking the bread and wine in the Christian sacrament of communion and protest the enforcement of the Texas law as an infringement of their right to worship God in their own way.

Strong economic considerations reinforce their protest. The peyote cactus grows most abundantly on the dry and rocky hills along the Rio Grande valley near Laredo, Texas, and is a bonanza to the owners of that land, since the buds sell for about $20.00 a thousand. Hitherto the Food and Drug Administration permitted the sale and use of peyote for "bona fide religious rites." According to the National Observer's report, hasty efforts will be made by lawmakers to repeal or modify the new law and so avoid violating the Indians' religious freedom.

In the light of our more recently acquired knowledge of the psychological side-effects of such delicacies as peyote and soma, we can read with greater understanding the ancient Greek tale of Glaucus, the fisherman, who ate a handful of grass growing in a meadow sloping to the sea, and experienced an irresistible impulse to leap into the sea. Our daily papers have reported many cases of LSD users irresistibly impelled to leap through plate-glass windows to their death in the street below. Glaucus' fate was happier. The sea-gods received him kindly, purged him of his human nature, and transformed him into a dolphin-tailed sea god himself. Happy, sportive sea-god he remained, although briefly saddened when the nymph Scylla spurned his love.

In a late hymn of the Rig Veda there is a description of a class of holy men called *Munis* or "the silent ones." They "wore the wind as a girdle" and could ride it as a bird can, but more important than that, they could read men's thoughts because they had partaken of the magic drink *Rudra*, which is a deadly poison for ordinary men.

The implications of Daniel's food habits, as described in the first chapter of the Book of Daniel, are not as crystal clear as

The Food Mystique

were the magic results of drinking Ruda as described in the Rig Veda. Daniel, in captivity, steadfastly refused to eat the meat of the king's table and insisted on eating pulse. However, it is not clear whether the reader is to conclude that a vegetarian diet makes one, like Daniel, very handsome and able to interpret men's minds, or that the peas and beans he ate had magic powers. Perhaps there is a still different meaning, namely that Daniel refused the meat of the king's table, which his fellow captives ate, because he knew it was tainted with evil, being, probably, the flesh of animals offered in sacrifice on unhallowed altars.

Another debatable point, this time about beans, concerns the reason for their prohibition as food in the Pythagorean brotherhood of ancient Greece. It has been suggested that Pythagoras was allergic to beans and, generalizing from his own experience with them, forbade them to his followers. It is more commonly assumed that abstaining from beans was a mandate for the order for religious rather than physiological reasons. The Pythagoreans were known to believe in the transmigration of souls, and beans were often thought to be the temporary way-stations of souls on their way to rebirth.

From early Hindu writings we have evidence of another interesting belief that connects food with the doctrine of transmigration of souls. There was a primitive Hindu conviction that conception occurred because either the husband or wife ate a fruit or vegetable into which a soul in transition had been dropped by the rain. In the Brdadaranyaka Upanishad the stages of transmigration are listed. Worthy souls, released by death, go first to the "World of the Fathers," the paradise of Yama, for a period of bliss. This they leave for a sojourn on the Moon. From the Moon, they float for a time in empty space, until upon contact with air they are caught up in rain and descend again to earth; there lodged in fruit or plants, they become food and are ready for rebirth. The wicked, without benefit of a period of bliss, are eaten by worms, birds, other animals, or even insects, to be reborn according to their just deserts.

No account of the food mystique could be considered adequate that fails to mention the connection of food with taboo.

Fasting as in Ramadan or in Lent or eating certain foods only as in the ritualistic observance of significant events such as the Passover are forms of taboo in essence resembling the "royal taboo" described by Freud in *Totem and Taboo*. He illustrates the potency of royal taboo by the account of the death, in terrible convulsions, of a healthy hungry young slave who, in ignorance, ate the remains of a royal banquet left by the roadside.

Frazer, writing of taboo, cites the case of a tinderbox last used by a Maori Chief. Several people, finding it and not knowing whose it was, lighted their pipes from it. When they discovered whose tinderbox it was, they all died of taboo—or fright; clear evidence, of course, that tinderboxes as well as cigarette packages should bear the label: "Caution, the contents may be dangerous."

There has been in these pages heretofore merely a hint of the deepest, strangest, most persistent belief about food—namely, the connection of food with death and with immortality. Egypt's ancient "Book of the Dead" made careful, ritualistic arrangements for the nourishment of a dead man's *ka* or soul. They thought the ka, not the mummy, which was preserved only that the ka might revisit it if it wished, needed everything it had needed while lodged in the living body: food, jewels, clothing, furniture. We have in our museums today great jars which mourning relatives kept filled with fresh wine for thirsty kas. Nor is the custom obsolete. A visitor to Japan today may happen upon a humble funeral procession in almost any fishing village. In the procession directly behind the mourner carrying the portrait of the deceased he may expect to see another mourner carrying a basket with loaves of freshly baked bread. They are food for the dead man's soul.

G.C. Atkins, in a truly remarkable book called *Procession of the Gods*, wrote in an introductory chapter called "Faiths of the Dark and the Dawn" that gifts to the dead are probably the germ of sacrifice, and tables spread for them may have supplied the earliest suggestion of communion with the unseen—along with fear and awe, and perhaps stronger than either or both, love of the dear dead may, he thinks, have convinced man of his membership in a second world with those he will not relinquish.

Mysticism, magic, and man's tenacious affection, coupled with

The Food Mystique

his blind resolve to believe the impossible if it coincides with his wishes, have combined to transform the cannibalistic act of eating another's body and drinking his blood into an act of worship. Today, countless worshippers believe in the power of bread and wine to be other than they seem and as spiritual food to nourish not the body but the soul, and not symbolically but literally to provide eternal life.

There are profound psychological reasons why an act connected with eating bread and drinking wine should become the awe-inspiring and sacred center of religious life. Eating and drinking are essential to physical well-being, to being as we say, "hale and hearty." It is only a short linguistic step from the Anglo-Saxon word *halig*, meaning to be well or whole, to our English word *holy*. That short step was taken centuries before our era by all the religions that accepted the premise that spiritual beings, like physical beings, needed nourishment. All the smoking altars of the past have wafted sustenance from the sacrificial victims to spiritual beings, whether gods or souls of the dead. The Egyptians provisioned their burial chambers not for the mummies wrapped in spicy cerements but for the kas, the souls released from their mummified bodies and visiting them only at will.

In parts of Europe and Asia where old traditions still linger, there is one proper and expected gift that friends bring to a home mourning a death. It is a loaf of freshly baked bread. The bas-relief from the family tomb of the Symmachorum of Roman fame shows in beautiful detail a priestess offering food and wine, presumably to the families' genius or tutelary god. The flame is already burning on the altar ready to lift the offering heavenward.

Thus the idea of spiritual food, implicit in the Eucharist, is an idea widely accepted and very old. It has remained for art to invest the act of consuming food as a necessity of survival with an aura of transcendant beauty. Few legends have the appeal of romantic attraction to equal those concerning the search for the Holy Grail, the chalice or some say the platter used by Christ at the last supper. As only the pure in thought and deed could approach it, the Grail became a religious symbol of great power.

Wherever in Christendom, whether at High Mass in a vast

cathedral or at a simple communion table in some small Protestant church, where the elements are homemade grape wine and a loaf baked by the deacon's wife, reverence cloaks the observance with solemn beauty. Nowhere, indeed, has man shown greater artistry than in transforming the inherently repulsive act of eating the body of another and drinking his blood into the supreme ritual of love.

CHAPTER V

The Greatest News Story in the Memory of Man

Some time during the Stone Age, in those mist-filled, indeterminate centuries, so easy to name, so difficult to locate exactly, and even more difficult to imagine, the Aryan ancestors of our North American Indians migrated from the region south of the Caucasus Mountains and carried with them the legend of a great flood that had happened long ago. They were one branch of a great scattering of people, which took centuries to move slowly, erratically, halfway around the world.

They went into Eastern Asia, probably to the north of the forbidding Himalayas, mingling their Aryan blood with the blood of yellow-skinned peoples by the way, and at last they entered North America over a land-bridge that, now partly submerged, forms the Aleutians.

It was probably some time between 3100 B.C. and 2000 B.C. that the first wave of this five or possibly seven-pronged migration, calling themselves Algonquins, crossed Canada to the Atlantic Coast. They were followed by the Iroquois, who swept across the Ohio and Hudson Valleys to southern New England. Later came the Delaware who settled in the valley of the Mississippi. They brought with them the *Walum-olum* of the Delawares. It was their sacred history, a world history consisting of picture-drawings, with 184 different symbols in wood telling of their sacred legends. There are five divisions of the Walum-olum, the first two of which tell of the creation of the world and of the great flood.

There is ample scientific confirmation that the deluge did occur, probably with the melting of polar ice-caps, indeed, that it probably will recur. The devastating waters undoubtedly covered much of the earth when the last glaciers melted, possibly around 10,000 B.C. The Mediterranean Ocean may be the last unevaporated pool left in its wake—what Australians would call a "billabong."

Leonard Woolley, an archeologist, in the 1920s excavated the site of the City of Ur on the Euphrates. We know Ur in the biblical account as the home of Abraham. In the upper levels of his excavations he made rich finds of royal graves that yielded much information about the ancient Sumerians of five thousand years ago. There it was he found the mosaic "standard of Ur," panels wrought with inlay in mother of pearl and lapis lazuli of tiny figures, which as eloquently as speech portray some details of that vanished world. His most amazing find, however, was that at forty feet down he came upon an alluvial deposit of clay over eight feet thick completely without shards. Obviously at some long distant time the waters of the Tigris-Euphrates estuary had backed up to cause a great floood. It was obvious to him that this was the flood of the Gilgamish Epic from which the account in Genesis was drawn.

The flood was the basis for the greatest news story of all time, passed along on the tongues of men for centuries, and in the telling becoming standardized but also, in isolated areas, acquiring minor embellishments that in turn tended to standardization. It was carved on clay tablets, chiseled into granite, preserved on wooden blocks, entrusted to manuscripts. It was translated in many languages, and always it was pruned or added to, shaped and interpreted by the tellers.

It takes little imagination to reconstruct those countless evenings in the centuries immediately following the flood when men with few or no words at their command told first by emotional sounds and gestures and then by increasing verbalization the story of the terrible flood. They may have told the story during a downpour, sitting in dim caves, as they watched it rain. They undoubtedly retold it, as they had heard it from their fathers, over campfires on hunting forays. Undoubtedly, too, the listeners, knowing the tale from childhood, added in choral fashion such significant details as "the animals two by two"; for forty days and forty

The Greatest News Story in the Memory of Man 49

nights"; "the rains fell and the depths of the sea were opened." They may have spoken words; they may have used gestures, but there is little need of invoking Jung's theory of racial memory, carried mysteriously in the blood stream, to explain the continuing life of the great story down the long years.

One can picture for himself the groups of ever-wandering people, small family groups, large tribal groups, now resting in a fertile valley, now driven by overpopulation or hostile neighbors to seek new homes in barren and forbidding places, and abiding ever briefly, a decade or a century or two; and again and again in the evening twilight the elders, with the children asking for a story, retelling the strange and dreadful story of the flood or the story of creation or speaking solemnly of a great spirit.

Thus we should not be surprised that the Chippewa Indians, a branch of the Delaware, have a tale of the flood, noticeably like the account of Genesis, which antedates any contact with Christian missionaries. It claims the flood engulfed the whole earth except the highest mountain tops where their ancestors were preserved.

The Algonquins, too, the first wave of migrants, brought their legends with them. They crossed Canada, until stopped by the Atlantic Ocean, and then turned south into what is now Maine and New Hampshire. In the White Mountains of New Hampshire, some of them chanced upon that majestic outcropping of rock to which Hawthorne gave the name "The Great Stone Face." The Algonquins recognized it as the great god, the great spirit of their legends. They may have seen it first on an autumn day when the sheer mountain slope below the face is mantled in the red and pink, the scarlet, the crimson, the orange and yellow gold of autumn. The result is a regal garment of Oriental splendor, fit for a great god.

These wanderers through time and space had brought with them the legend of a great god, "the Sky Father." He has been called by countless names such as Manu-pitar, Javeh, Ahura-Mazda, Zeus, Aton, Jupiter, Brahma, which all signify a great spirit. And in the benign profile sharp and clear against an azure sky the Algonquins recognized "The Great Spirit" they had hitherto worshipped unseen. Here in the White Mountains they had come face to face with it.

The serene face looked not at them but beyond them as they gazed up at it, and into the misty blue of space. It must have added to the awe with which they regarded the face, the embodiment of the majesty and power of the Great Sky Father, that if they moved a few paces to the right, or to the left, or attempted to climb toward it, the wondrous face vanished, and they could see only a rough outcropping of bare crags where it had been. Yet even as they moved back again, still regarding the bleak and massive escarpment where the face had been, it was there once more; remote, austere, immense and yet serene, undeniably the face of a god. It was a god who permitted himself to be seen at a certain place, at a discreet distance, and otherwise vanished into the crags of the mountain.

We can share the awe these children of migrants from beyond the Caucasus must have felt at the confrontation. Their god, until now a legend, had shown himself to them. He dwelt with them in the lofty heights of this new, unpeopled wilderness, now their home. The great mysterious face must have confirmed their belief in the record in the Walum-olum of creation and the flood. Here in the White Mountains of a strange new world they found the Sky Father of ancient legend, a great spirit whose benevolent face could appear in all its majesty and disappear with all suddenness if they dared to approach nearer. Surely both legends must be true. Indeed, in their wanderings they must have heard now and again distorted versions of the time of the great waters told by strange peoples evidently ignorant of the true happenings as told to their fathers by their fathers' fathers long, long ago in a faraway land.

The story of the flood as told in Genesis is a vivid tale full of belief-inducing, practical details, specific measurements, and definite time intervals. Take the ark, for instance. Any Boy Scout troop with a good scoutmaster, materials supplied by the Chamber of Commerce, and a convenient and spacious back yard could build the three-storied ark with a door on one side. God's timely warning to Noah, a righteous man in a totally wicked world,

The Greatest News Story in the Memory of Man

seems just and kind—unless one stops to question the depravity of babes-in-arms, kittens and puppies and young sportive lambs, all doomed to death by drowning.

In the excitement of the loading, one readily dismisses doubts about the provisioning and housing of a pair of every living thing in so circumscribed a craft. One waits in suspense for the return of the birds sent forth to explore and rejoices with Noah and his family that the waters finally subsided. Not even "Jack and the Bean Stalk" is a better bedtime story.

The same great disaster was handed down by the Greeks in oral form and finally found its way into written legend. But the deluge of Greek myth is a less detailed and adequate bedtime story than the story of Noah and the Ark. However, it has its points.

The Greek account of the deluge, like the Hebrew version of the flood, is a moral tale. It begins with the wickedness of all the dwellers on the face of the earth. The Father of men and the gods, in this case Zeus, decided to wipe them out and start over. Poseidon, God of the Sea, helped Zeus to try to exterminate the human race by drowning. Very effective were the torrents of rain and the rising waters they unleashed in the relatively short space of nine days and nights. It was no time at all compared to one hundred and fifty days of rising water in the Hebrew story followed by a full forty days of receding water and another fourteen before the dove returned to the Ark with an olive branch in leaf.

That Zeus and Poseidon did not completely destroy the human race was due to the foresight of a benevolent demi-god Prometheus, the same who risked eternal torment by stealing fire from the very hearth of Heaven to bring man comfort. Prometheus warned his son, Deucalion, to build a great wooden chest, provision it, and secrete his wife Pyrrha in it. After the nine days and nights of tossing in turbulent water, the chest with the husband and wife, basically unharmed, but doubtless bruised, came to rest, not as in the Genesis story on Mt. Ararat, but on the highest peak of Parnassus, which alone was not overwhelmed. Deucalion and Pyrrha were utterly alone in a dead world. No animals "two by two" trooped wtih them from the chest. As they emerged in terror from it, they veiled their heads and entered a slime-covered temple they found on the mountain slope. There they prayed to the gods for help. In answer to their prayers they received strange instructions for the recreation of mankind. They were to descend the mountain and throw "the bones of their mother" over their shoulders as they went. Their mother was earth, but her bones? They thought they might be the stones scattered all about them. They were right. The stones Deucalion cast behind him became men; those thrown by Pyrrha became women.

And the Chinese, at about the same time as the Greeks, had a different way of telling the story of the flood. According to their story, Sago—King Yu—a Chinese Noah, benevolent, good, and very wise, saved not just himself and his family, but people in the country at large who listened to his warnings.

The story of the flood was told in places far distant from each other and told again and again. It was told in Babylon at about the same time it was told in China. Scholars have recently discovered that the Hittites knew the legend of the flood before the Babylonians. The Babylonian version occurs in the eleventh canto of the Gilgamesh Epic written upon clay tablets about two thousand years before Christ. The tablets were written in the ancient city of Nippur, and their philosophy is thought to have inspired the sophisticated writer of the Book of Ecclesiastes in the Old Testament. "Vanity of vanities, saith the preacher: vanity of vanities, all is vanity." The teaching of the Gilgamesh epic is that, as the gods are many and capricious and life is short, one should live happily with one's wife and children. One should enjoy life to the utmost, wearing bright garments of soft texture and eating good food. The people of Nippur speculated as to the origin of things; the origin of individual things such as trees and men and the origin and destiny of the universe. They were advised by their teachers to give up the quest for immortality.

It was not until 1872 that George Smith, a self-taught student of cuneiform characters who was at the time a humble assistant in the Egyptian-Assyrian section of the British Museum, began to decipher the tablets Hormuzd Rassam had sent to the

The Greatest News Story in the Memory of Man

Museum. Slowly, with infinite pains, he translated the story of the hero Gilgamesh, only to discover that the story broke off at its very climax in the Rassam tablets.

With a thousand guineas offered by the London Daily Telegraph, Smith set off to Mesopotamia to excavate at Kuyunjik for the missing clay tablets to complete the Gilgamesh Epic. He brought home 384 fragmented clay tablets, among them the tablets with the story of the flood. It was an astounding and enlightening archeological find.

It was while on the quest for immortality that the hero of the epic, Gilgamesh of Uruk, heard the story of the flood from his kinsman Ut Napishtim. In many ways this account resembles the Noah story. Family together with wild beasts and domesticated cattle are crowded into the ship. The storm in all its fury resembles the Biblical storm. But there was a significant addition to the story. The gods, too, were in danger of drowning in the flood, which was caused not by man's wickedness, but by a bitter quarrel between Isthar, the queen and wife of Anu, and Enlil, who sought to use the flood to kill her.

During the flood the gods themselves suffered fear and cold and hunger. We are told that "The gods themselves were dismayed at the flood. They retreated, they went up to the heaven of Anu. The gods cowered like dogs, they crouched by the walls."

Then, as in the Noah version, after the ship bumped against a mountain side and the storm subsided, birds were released. First a dove went to and fro but returned to the ship; a swallow followed, but it too returned. A raven, on being released, came near the ship, wading and croaking, but it did not return. Thereupon the people were released from the ship and at once offered a sacrifice for their deliverance. At this, there was rejoicing among the half-starved gods, for the epic states that "The gods smelt the sweet savor, the gods gathered like flies about him that offered up the sacrifice."

In the translation recorded in the *Sacred Books of the World* by A. C. Bouquet, a Pelican Book, Ishtar thereupon made the following dramatic pronouncement as she raised the great jewel which Anu had made according to her wish:

> These, gods—by the lapis lazuli upon my neck—I
> Will not forget!
> These days will I bear in mind, and never more forget
> Let the gods come to the offering
> But let not Enlil come to the offering,
> For as much as he took no counsel, but caused the flood
> And delivered my people to destruction.

This does not exhaust the store of legends about the great flood, and one additional account from India's Bhagavad Gita is too important to be omitted. It recounts the part played at the time of the flood by the great Hindu god Vishnu. Devotees of Vishnu regard him as the creative aspect of Brahma, the source of the universe and of all created things, including man. He strives endlessly to preserve and protect his creation. To this end, at times of crisis, he has again and again incarnated himself in a human being or an animal in order to come to the rescue. Every hero or great man has been a partial incarnation of the god, and at least ten times the incarnation has been total.

At the time of the deluge, Vishnu took the form of a great horned fish. First, however, he warned Manu, a good and righteous man, of the impending danger, and then he propelled the ship in which Manu, his family, and seven wise men had taken refuge by means of a rope attached to the bow of the ship and fastened to the horn on his head.

An important loss during the height of the storm that caused the flood necessitated a second incarnation on the part of Vishnu. The jar of nectar by which the gods preserved their youth had been swept into the ocean. To regain it, Vishnu became a tortoise and swam to the very bottom of the ocean. The other gods erected a mountain on his back and around the mountain twined the great snake Vasuki. Then they churned the ocean by twirling the mountain. This vast churning brought up the lost nectar from the ocean's depth. The gods were already immortal, but the nectar, now happily restored, assured them eternal youth as well.

Anyone reflecting on the varying news reports of the world's major cosmic disaster cannot fail to notice the difference made

The Greatest News Story in the Memory of Man

in the telling by the reporters' views of history. He may, as did the unknown reporter in the Book of Genesis or the Greek author of the story of Deucalion and Pyrrha, see divine despair at human wickedness as the motive for unleashing the cleansing flood, or see it as in the Gilgamesh Epic as a chance incident due to the capricious enmities of the gods. In the first view, cosmic history becomes a vast divine plan in which moral considerations interact with physical laws. In the second view, there is no "divine far-off event toward which the whole creation moves." In it there are no punishments for thwarting the plan, but also no security, as a whim, a passing quarrel of the gods, can bring destruction to all created things.

As for the rainbow, which in Genesis God spoke of to Noah as the sign of his covenant that the waters shall never again become a flood to destroy all flesh, neither those who believe the universe is vulnerable to capricious whim nor sober men of science see it as God's luminous signature. Yet, all men after a summer storm can, however, view the vaulting radiance of its great band of color and experience in its mysterious beauty that leaping of the heart we know when hope is renewed.

CHAPTER VI

The Mortal Gods

We speak so naturally of "the immortal gods" or simply of "the immortals" as equivalent to Gods, or of one God, eternal, "the same yesterday and today and forever," that we tend to overlook the mortal gods. Yet the many dying gods of the world have inspired deepest devotion.

Moreover, it is through the recurring legends of the many dying gods who have inspired love as well as worship that a student of world religion becomes aware that man since the beginning of story-telling has told his children one great story over and over, time and again. He has changed the names, he has varied the incidents, but the central character is the same. He is always a god who is a dying hero. In some of the tellings that is sufficient. Each god is a poignant comment on the transitoriness of even the most precious in life. In other legends the mortal god is a savior god as well. And finally, it is quite possible that not a few of them were first of all mortal men who nobly won an immortality of remembrance from their peers and by dying will always live.

Their names are legion, but to call the roll of but a few of them will indicate their deep significance in world religion. Because, as man forms his conception of the mortal gods, he attempts also to fathom his belief in his own immortality, they continue to be central in religious practice.

One of the early mortal gods of whom we have knowledge, Tammus, was worshipped in ancient Babylon. His death, theme of the "Lament of the Flute for Tammus," left his wife, Ishtar, and his devotees desolate, even as the death of summer leaves the world barren and bleak. But Ishtar's exceeding love for Tammus brought him back from the world of the dead, not once but

The Mortal Gods

many times. Even as spring and its warm sunshine return to a frozen earth, so Tammus returned.

Ezekiel, stern prophet of Jehovah, heard the voices of the women of Israel joining with the voices of the women of Babylon in their lament for Tammus. In the eighth chapter of Ezekiel there is an account that as Ezekiel sat in his house, on the fifth day of the sixth month of the sixth year, a fiery apparition came before him and put forth a hand and lifted him by a lock of his head to deposit him by the gate of the Lord's house in Jerusalem. Behold! There sat the "women of Israel weeping for Tammus." Ezekiel denounced this abomination vehemently. God's terrible punishment followed swiftly. He promised that therefore he would also deal in fury with the idolators: "Mine eyes shall not spare neither will I have pity: and though they cry in mine ears with a loud voice, yet will I not hear them." Thus, in the words of Ezekiel, does Jehovah deal with nature worship.

Tammus, the young and beautiful mortal god of Babylon, was known by different names in neighboring countries. Ishtar, too, was known by other names. In Egypt she was Isis and Tammus was Osiris. In Syria he became Adon, and his river, the Adonis, still flows seaward from Syria. Ishtar was also Astarte, or Ashteroth, and her husband Baal, a sun god and god of fertility, is hard to distinguish from Adon.

Modern tourists visiting Byblos on the Mediterranean, because it is on the site of a number of older cities in various stages of excavation, can by scrambling to the top of the ruined Crusader's castle look down on a series of ruins at their feet. One looks into the past centuries as one views the remnants of a Roman amphitheater and, not far from it, the pillars of a Greek temple. Beneath the level of the Roman and the Greek ruins are clearly visible traces of the Phoenician civilization that antedated them. The massive stone blocks forming the harbor entrance and lining its sheer cliffs are pock-marked with time and worn smooth under foot by the tread of merchant seamen from the days when Assyria was a great nation to the present. These stones echoed in the Phoenician past to cries of sorrow for the death of Adon, symbol of youth, of sunlight, and of the eternal renewal of life. It is better not to ask what bloody sacrifices may have been made within sight of these same stones to the god who was also a god of fertility.

As life's most precious treasures and life's most poignant sorrows were embodied in the person of every slender, dying god, it was small wonder that each time the god died, his bereft wife and all her followers and his were faithful at his altar. Rome knew the legend of Adon and Itar, or Adones and Astarte in the tale of Attis and Cybele. Sometimes Attis' name is spelled Atys and Cybele is known also as Rhea, mother of the Olympian gods, or as "Great Mother of the Gods." Her ancient home was Phrygia, although she travelled to many lands, and her priests were called *corybantes*.

The corybantes celebrated Cybele's festivals with wild dances and orgiastic rites. At one such rite, a pale and beautiful lad named Atys, whom Cybele loved more than her other worshippers, was trampled to death at the foot of a pine tree sacred to her. The pine tree received his spirit, and violets sprang up from his blood. On the third day after his violent death, he returned to life; the rejoicing of Cybele's worshippers, intoxicated with springtime and their own youth, knew no bounds. The story of Atys is very like the story of Dionysus whom in many ways he resembles. The names change, but essentially the same story of violent death, deep grief, resurrection of a hero-god, and wild rejoicing has repeated itself through the centuries in lands as different from each other as Syria, Egypt, Greece, and Rome.

The Egyptian account of Isis and Osiris merits retelling, and in fact it has been retold in many languages and in many ages, with changes of incidents, but with strict adherence to the central theme, which our Quaker poet Whittier wove into his New England poem "Snowbound." He wrote that "Life is ever lord of Death, and Love can never wholly lose its own."

Like other Egyptian gods, Osiris appeared in various roles. He was the creator-god and was himself self-created. Mankind sprang from his tears. Whole dynasties of Gods were his offspring. Osiris was King of the Gods, the husband of Isis and the brother of Set. Set was evil incarnate, a dark and treacherous god bent on Osiris'

The Mortal Gods

destruction. Osiris, young and beautiful King of the Gods, rejoicing in the adoration of his sister-wife, Isis, had the radiance of the sun in his face. Being guileless, he suspected no guile and was easily tricked and slain by Set, the clever betrayer, the God of the Darkness. After the murder, Isis mourned without ceasing, but also without ceasing she sought the mutilated corpse of her adored husband. She finally found and reassembled the parts of his severed body and thus restored him to life. This happened not once only, but was repeated even as winter conquers the fruitful time of growth and harvest, and earth becomes frozen into barrenness, until spring once more returns in an unending mystic cycle.

As King of the Dead, Osiris appeared grave and stern, yet he was still beloved more than feared, for he promised a return to the joy of living. When in ancient Egypt a man died, it became customary to prefix to his given name the name of the god. It meant far more than we mean, when on like occasions we use "late" in the same manner. The "late John Brown" falls far short of meaning what "Osiris-John Brown" would have implied in Egypt. Osiris was the promise of ever renewed life. The word as a prefix assured man his place in the recurrent cycles of being: the cycles of dawn after darkness, spring after winter, and the precious miracle of hope after despair.

The Egyptians were tolerant of, even hospitable to, new gods, and many new gods joined Isis and Osiris. Those whose names have survived in clay or on stone or on papyrus number in the hundreds. For the most part, only their names survived; not so in the case of Isis and Osiris. They were so deeply established in the affections of the Egyptians that they migrated with them, suffering a change of name but not of nature, as war, or trade, or migration took Egyptians into Greece and later to Rome. There are prayers and hymns and speeches in the Egyptian "Book of the Dead" that were incorporated into the ritual of the Greek mystery cults. They echo today in contemporary liturgies around the world.

Dionysus, whom many consider Osiris, as he was reborn in Greece, was a young god of wine and song. He, too, was a beloved god who suffered death—he was torn limb by limb by devoted followers—and later he was reborn. In Greece, his mysteries and those later associated with Osiris had much in common. They and the mysteries named for other gods were the means of religious expression for the Greek and, later, the Roman masses.

The Olympian gods were far away and very self-centered, but the mysteries were irresistible, partly because they were secret and required an initiation, but mostly because they promised the uneducated peasants and enslaved city-dwellers a ray of hope—the hope of a future life in a paradise of freedom and plenty. It is a matter of history that devotees embraced the rites of the mysteries, which were often orgies, and the god in whose name they were held with delirious joy. From the sixth century B.C. the mysteries flourished in the Graeco-Roman world. In the first century after Christ they were still powerful, and through the mystery connected with Mithras, a savior-god, greatly influenced Christianity.

It is highly probable that the unrestrained bestiality of some of the mysteries, such as many associated with the worship of Cybele, may be expressing itself still in the flagellation—amounting to human sacrifice —practised by the most primitive and fanatic of the Indians of New Mexico. The religious orgies of the Cybelean mysteries were begun by a long-continued, relentless beating of drums, augmented by deafening clashing of cymbals and shrieking of flutes. The devotees whirled in a convulsive dance until, almost exhausted, they suddenly began slashing at their own bodies with swords. The participants felt they had attained a moment of divinity, their release from human bondage, in the state of emotional insensitivity to pain induced by the wild, continuous music, the hypnotic dancing, and near exhaustion. Only the most fantastically devout achieved these heights, but even the rank and file of Cybele's followers could attain immortality by less painful, but exceedingly gruesome rites.

There was, for instance, in the Cybelian rites of initiation the ordeal of the Tauroboleum. The initiate was put in a pit covered by widely spaced heavy planks. A consecrated bull was slaughtered on the planks and as its blood gushed and then dripped down upon the initiate, he had to drink it, bathe in it, wallow in it.

The Mortal Gods

Of course, it was primitive magic, a dramatic reaffirmation of the belief that the immortality of the god could be transferred to a sacred animal, in this case the bull, and that the worshipper by washing himself with its blood and imbibing it could win immortality by washing away his sin and guilt.

Many legends grew up about Attis, lover of Cybele, whose counterpart was known earlier under various names, Tammus, Adonis, Osiris among them. He was reported to have been born miraculously of a virgin. He died of self-immolation, and three days later was reborn. His death and his resurrection were celebrated annually in Rome. The festival began with a solemn day of sorrow commemorating the death of Attis, the young god, and after three days reached a climax of joy to celebrate his rebirth.

But the strongest, purest mystery cult to grip the Roman populace was the cult of Mithras, introduced from Persia about the first century before Christ and dominant in Rome for over three hundred years.

Mithras, also written Mithra or Mitra, was one of the Aryan gods mentioned in the Vedas. He was a sun god, guardian of day, and associated with Varuna—a very great god of the first order who ruled the night and judged men's acts. Varuna was often regarded as the source of cosmic order and hence a creator god, while Mithra's province was to act as guardian of vows and contracts.

The Persian Mithras whose mystery cult was introduced into Rome had a somewhat different history, for he began as a hero who later became a god, absorbing in the process many of the duties and aspects of Mithra of the Vedas. About Mithras' miraculous birth, a story grew up that it was witnessed by a few shepherds who had journeyed to the spot to be present with gifts for the child.

Mithras' supreme deed was to risk and lose his life in a fight with a sacred bull. When the terrible struggle ended, both lay dying. The blood of the slain bull gave renewed life to the earth, and in dying Mithras himself gained immortality. From the 'Abode of Light" he now, with Ahura-Mazda, watched over his **faithful.**

Even Zoroaster's triumphant religious reform that enthroned Ahura-Mazda as the Almighty God of Light, could not wean the populace from their love of Mithras, whom they continued to worship as a champion of the Sun-God against the God of Darkness.

When the cult of Mithras, by way of Babylon and Greece, finally reached Rome, the bright, strong warrior-god, triumphant in his death, had instant appeal for the war-weary men of the Roman legions. He became their own representative and guarantee of a future life. They could identify with him, and as members of his cult gave him full allegiance. Mithraism had the strength and appeal of all cosmic religions of earth and sky.

According to Lewis Browne, as stated in his book *This Believing World,** there are to this day along the Danube and in Northern Africa certain caves in which there are statues and carvings depicting scenes from the life of Mithras. These caves were once churches where followers of Mithras three times daily and most elaborately on the day sacred to the sun and on the 25th of December observed prescribed ritual. The ritual included pouring of libations, ringing of bells, chanting of hymns, and the lighting of candles. Above all, the ritual demanded a communal meal of the blood and flesh of a sacramental animal. We would call it a mass. The participants believed this ritual united them with their Lord Mithras. It is easy to see that Christianity absorbed much from the worship of Mithras in a struggle for supremacy that lasted well to the end of the second century after Christ, a fact substantiated by archeological findings along the Rhine where Roman legions brought his worship.

Undoubtedly, Christianity was enabled to win in the struggle against the followers of Mithras partly because it too could offer a savior-god, who had known death and through his triumph over death could bestow immortality, and partly because, like almost every victorious religion in the history of man, it was able to absorb much from its rival. Old festival days might still be celebrated but with a new purpose; candles lighted, but to a new hope. The

---

*New York: Macmillan Co., 1944.

The Mortal Gods

25th of December, the winter solstice by ancient reckoning, which had been celebrated as the birthday of Mithras, a sun god, was equally joyous when celebrated as the nativity of Jesus. It was still the time when shepherds had arrived with gifts for a newborn child. Thus in the assimilation of the cult of Mithras into Christian worship, time once more rendered tribute meant for one god to a new god, his successful rival.

Two men, both well-born and roughly contemporary, became the arch heretics of the Hindu faith. Both denied the existence of the many Hindu gods, the efficacy of prayer, and the need for a priesthood. Perhaps they had been influenced by the nihilistic philosophy of the Upanishads. At any rate, they were both philosophical thinkers. One was Prince Mahavira, the founder of Jainism; the other, forty years his junior, was Siddharta Gautama, the son of a wealthy rajah in the Valley of the Ganges. He founded Buddhism. Though both denied the existence of the gods, both were eventually deified by devout followers and preside today over altars in glittering temples, inhaling the fragrance of incense and of flowers. Their followers are numbered in the millions, and their influence has circled the globe.

Since ancient times there has been a tendency to associate religion with medicine and the healing arts. Undoubtedly the troubled, anxious minds of men have wanted more than a teacher and a leader. They could accept nothing short of a god to lean upon. Safe in his arms they lost their anxiety. They were healed of their fear. The power of physical healing is also a mark of divinity.

There were many parallels in their lives and in their teaching, but Mahavira stopped far short of Gautamas' ethical insight. Each until manhood lived a life of opulence and ease; each of them renounced it. Mahavira became an ascetic and after twelve years reached a Nirvana of salvation through his self-denial. Then, he journeyed through India with his gospel of self-salvation. "Man, thou art thine own friend." Wilfull self-destruction was the sole duty one owed oneself. One's sole legitimate desire was for non-being; death by starvation was man's ultimate triumph. There were other subordinate details of his teaching such as doing no injury to any living being, hating no one, loving no one. There was room for one minor emotion: his followers could feel scorn for women. The burning central core of his message as the "Conqueror," the "Jina," was self-annihilation. He was born in 599 B.C. and died when 70 in strict accordance with his doctrine, a gentle anchorite whose utter sincerity and courage drew men to him in admiration. Soon, legends of a miraculous birth and miraculous death grew up about him. By the year 400 B.C. he was worshipped as a god. To this day worshippers kneel at his altars in prayer. The most glittering temple in Calcutta is the Jain temple, set in exquisite gardens and sought by an endless procession of people seeking his aid.

The world is well acquainted with the historical details of the other teacher who became a god. They have heard how Siddharta Gautama stole out of his palace by night, leaving his young wife and newborn son asleep, but he did not at once become a hermit like Mahavira. First, he joined a group of philosophers, cave dwellers like the hermits, it is true, but not ascetics. Their self-denial was their exclusive devotion to speculative conversation about the nature of reality, or Brahma. They sought by words to probe the metaphysical Mystery of Being, and the young prince soon wearied of what he realized was a sham battle against windmills. Then he, like Mahavira before him, with five fellow truth-seekers took the bitter road of austere self-mortification. For six years, he persisted in seeking salvation through pain. Some days he allowed himself a single grain of rice. Devout Buddhists often gaze upon a carved image of a starving Buddha as devout Christians look upon a crucifix. "He was acquainted with grief." Unlike Mahavira, Gautama did not reach salvation by the road of asceticism. At last, deeply depressed, stiting quietly under the famous bo tree near Benaris, he had a sudden insight. Henceforth, he was the Buddha, the Enlightened One, the Great Teacher.

What he taught was a morality, wise and profound, based on moderation, much like Aristotle's "Golden Mean." He based his philosophy of conduct on "Four Noble Truths" concerning human nature and prescribed for conduct the Eightfold Noble Path of "Right Belief, Right Resolve, Right Speech, Right Action, Right

The Mortal Gods

Livelihood, Right Effort, Right Thought, and Right Meditation." He had realized that Nirvana is not a state of being but a state of mind and actually inaugurated a mental hygiene movement in the cause of happiness and morality. Followers came slowly, and there were periods of waning interest even after his death and then, as it happened to Mahavira it happened to him. He was followed not because he was a teacher with great wisdom but because he was a god with authority. It is always easier for untutored masses to accept the power of an authority than the logic of a thinker, easier to be loyal to a god than to a teacher.

Gautama's heretical doctrines were incisive and inclusive. Of god he said: "Who is there has ever seen Brahma face to face?" Of prayer he said: "Could the farther bank of the river Akirvati come over to this side, no matter how much a man prayed it to do so?" As for the soul, he said it was just a name for the totality of human desires and dies when the body dies. He explained it by an analogy: the chariot no longer exists when the wheels, shaft, axle, carriage, and banner-staff are removed. So all the worry about transmigration is worry about a myth. He used exactly the same argument Epicurus used to dismiss the fear of death in the Greek world—"When we are, death is not; when death is, we are not." Having cleared away the superstitions of religion, Gautama enunciated the positive moral teaching that he made a religion: "The Law of Karma." The deed lives on. Every deed has a consequence.

But by the third century B.C., Buddhism had become no longer a philosophy of life, but a religion. Like most religions with a learned priesthood, it split into rival factions. The newest sect, called the Mahayana or the Greater Raft or the Greater Vehicle (it is translated both ways in English), said of Gautama that the "Blessed One" had been divine from the first. He had been supernaturally conceived. From the moment of his birth he had been a wise and wondrous babe, and the birth itself was attended by miraculous happenings. His life had been sinless. After his death, according to orthodox doctrine, he has been regularly reincarnated in certain holy men called Bodhisattvas, savior gods sent to earth at times of earth's great need.

Later, even the Hinayana sect, a chronologically earlier form of Buddhism, surrendered to the god-theory, and Nirvana became again for all Buddhists a heaven, not as Buddha taught, a state of mind, and could be reached by ritualistic kissing of the toe of a great bronze image of Buddha. Today prayer-wheels spin in Buddhist temples around the world, and saffron-robed young priests present their begging bowls at the locked gates of the compounds of wealthy merchants in Bangkok so that these merchants, through charity, may save their individual souls.

Strangely alone among the mortal gods whom men have loved, stands the Norse god Balder, the fair, the beautiful, the gifted, beloved by all—by all but one, the envious and evil Loki. He did not die to save mankind but was slain in a merry jest by the fatal stab of a branch of mistletoe placed in his blind friend Hoder's unsuspecting hands by evil Loki. He has no altars, no devoted worshippers, no shrines, no hymns of praise. He stands in men's memory, a lonely monument to Death and to that law of being that ordains that death cannot be circumvented.

And yet he is very much of the company of the mortal gods. Sir James Frazer, author of *The Golden Bough*, uncovered a practise common in early society. Certain tribes regularly sacrificed not scapegoats, but the chief's own son, the crown prince, their darling and their pride, to propitiate the gods whose anger was so nearly implacable.

As the rising fever of autumn's leaves foretold the imminent death of the year and primitive men remembered winter with its storms and bitter cold, they made their offerings to heaven. They were not like the offerings of the Pilgrims on the New England Coast, thank-offerings out of gratitude. They were offerings of supplication made out of fear. If Sir James Frazer's surmise is correct, the names of the princes and the heroes who fell sacrificial victims for their people lived on in legend. Through the centuries they lost their mortal connotation and acquired through religious poetry and art that high heaven of immortality where Plato says Pure Beauty dwells in a world incorruptible and permanent. And there one finds Balder.

CHAPTER VII

Pattern

The argument from design, namely, that the presence of pattern in the universe implies a divine designer, is the most venerable argument for the existence of God, but it is not the concern of this chapter. It has been stated, analyzed and weighed many times in the past, perhaps most competently by Immanuel Kant.

Here, noting and accepting the infinite variety of fixed and dependable patterns, each capable in turn of being an element in other patterns, the purpose is rather to explore the significance attached to the presence of pattern, or order, as found in experience by the religions of the world. The specific question raised is whether the religion in question equates universal law with deity, or regards it as superior to and antedating its god or gods, or looks upon it as a creation of deity There are religions that give clearcut answers to this problem and make the answer their central religious truth. There are others that waver between different answers.

Pattern, form, law, order, these words used as synonyms call for definition. To say that they *emerge* from chaos or confusion is not to say much. But it is a significant beginning. The great writer of the first chapter of Genesis saw clearly that creation was a function of arrangement. The earth emerged as God separated sea and land; day and night emerged as he separated light from darkness. The "dry land" of the Book of Genesis was a new pattern from out of chaos, just as the sea was a novelty, a creation.

We are constantly engaged in the production of new patterns in our daily lives, because the problems we meet consist of data not yet properly related. A problem lacks form and is devoid of meaning except as a challenge and/or a thwarting. Out of a plethora of sense data we strive to produce a meaningful whole.

The "meaningful whole" emerges just as the pattern square that was in no sense 'in" the matches emerges when four of them are placed end to end in a certain way. From the same matches a line could emerge. Thus order or pattern or meaning in human experience is an emergent due to intellectual mastery.

Patterns are as many and as varied as are our needs. There is for example, the casual pattern of "this and therefore that" which a child must learn to see in order to survive. When a child has grown to manhood, he still spends much of his life learning to recognize patterns. As a child, he discovered his own growth pattern with eager delight: "When I'm a little older," he proclaimed with confidence. Later as a naturalist he may observe the growth pattern of a redwood tree, with its sudden initial thrust of energy and the majestic arc of its long, slow decline. Or he may describe the life pattern of a crocus with its quick response to the warm rains of spring and its equally brief enjoyment of the sun. He may, like Spengler, explore the patterns called *epigonies* and generalize concerning the birth and death of civilizations.

If a child is fortunate in his education, he may learn from the configuration of snowflakes that infinite variety and individuality are compatible with strict limitation. If he has a mentor as wise as Confucius, he will learn that happiness consists in willing conformity to the proper patterns in human relationships.

If a child, on reaching his maturity, becomes a scientist, a theologian, or a philosopher, he will spend his strength searching for the fundamental, but often hidden and elusive, relationships which pattern human experience. Whether he is an economist or a meteorologist, a statesman or a chemist, he seeks to find law or ultimate pattern. If he is seeking to find God, he may find him through an astronomer's telescope in the stupendous ordering of space or in the hitherto inscrutable biological sequences that begin to yield to scientific probing under man's fascinated but apprehensive gaze.

The primary concern of natural science, from astronomy to nuclear physics, is to disclose the intricate patterns of the universe. Scientists map the heavens, and scientists may also analyze the structural relationships of subatomic particles. Dr. Murray Gell-

Pattern

Mann of the California Institute of Technology has named these latter relationships "the eightfold way," and in doing so, was obviously mindful of the parallel to Buddha's analysis of the pattern or "way" that marks the good-life.

Philosophy in all its differing aspects such as cosmological, religious, metaphysical, ethical is equally as concerned with order, system, law, or what I call pattern, as we are in everyday living or in pure science. It was the concern of the earliest Greek cosmologists, even as it is of a contemporary social anthropologist, Professor Claude Levi-Strauss of the College de France. Among the early Greek philosophers concerned with the concept of pattern, one thinks inevitably of Pythagoras (572-497 B.C.) with his doctrine that "numbers," that is, mathematical relationships, are the basis and essence of the qualities of things. Incidentally, he was interested in music and discovered the octave, noting the relationship between the length of a plucked string and the number of its vibrations with the quality of pitch.

Levy-Strauss, the contemporary philosopher who calls himself a structuralist, holds that the human intellect has as permanent a structure or pattern, as water has with its two molecules of hydrogen and one of oxygen. As the pattern of the intellect is as fixed as the pattern a nuclear physicist studies in the atom, our perception of the universe is equally limited and fixed. Inevitably it means also that we discover only those patterns we are equipped to discover.

This modern structuralism is essentially a reaffirmation of the teaching of Immanuel Kant. In his *Critique of Pure Reason* Kant demonstrated that thinking is essentially putting sense data into a certain limited number of categories. The two indispensable categories or patterns are time and space. Even "the light that never was on land or sea" is negatively related to time and space, and beyond that you have to take the poet's word for it that it was the "inspiration and a poet's dream." It might just as well be, in fact is, an X. We cannot think intelligently of something that is forever nonexistent, i.e., somthing we have no apparatus for grasping. Kant considered the categories of time and space the prerequisites or presuppositions of understanding. He held that the capacity to have experience of a spatial and temporal nature is an *a priori* characteristic of the knower, a characteristic that however at the same time puts limits to his knowing. His *Critique of Pure Reason* included also a study of the other innate patterns, which today we would call "programmings," of the human mind that determine the capacities and the limits of human reasoning. His conclusion was that everywhere in the sensible world we experience only what can be fitted into the inborn patterns of our mind. In a word, the order we find in experience, we ourselves introduce.

Anticipating the age of computers by nearly two hundred years, Kant described man's intellect as a unit innately programmed, which could receive raw data through the senses and issue them as knowledge, i.e., as meaningfully connected by categories within the limits of its programming. In addition to the presuppositions of time and space, Kant named four other categories, drawn from the classifications of logic, that he considered basic. They were: quantity, quality, relation, and modality. Each of these was further subdivided. Quality could be specified in terms of reality, negation, limitation; and relation as substance and inherence, causality and dependence, and reciprocity. Finally, modality yielded in Kant's analysis the three minor classifications of possibility, existence, and negation.

Many thinkers since Kant have acknowledged their debt to him, even while challenging the final adequacy of his essentially mechanical conception of man as a robot computer. John Dewey's philosophy, for instance, taking into account the physiological findings of stimulus-response psychology, built on the idea of the human brain as a programmed computer. Kant had written of an intellect with innate categories; Dewey wrote of a brain programmed or modified by experience.

Dewey's account of "meaning" and its origin begins with the physiological findings that stimuli initiate nerve impulses from sense organs to response mechanisms through the central nervous system, where they encounter synaptic connections, pliable enough to be broached, firm enough to retain a trace of the passage of the impulse in terms of lowered resistance. Thus pro-

Pattern

gramming begins, but it is retained only if accompanied by satisfaction. Painful results set up a negative pattern that increases synaptic resistance to a disaster-terminated pattern. The burnt child, Dewey reminded the world, does not again put his hand in the fire, but shrinks from it. A robot child with a mind innately programmed, once and for all, could only repeat his disastrous performance.

The emergence of meaning through experience, the constant discovery of novel aspects of things, is not an argument for the absence of order in the universe, but merely points to our blindness to patterns of many kinds because of limited experience. Each day to which we awake is a new day. We cannot, as Heraclitus said, step twice in the same river. Yet in spite of the expanding novelty of living, we fall back to rest in the comfortable assurance of sameness, or enduring order. In the final analysis, we do not so much create order as discover it. We come face to face with patterned reality as Buddha in his moment of enlightenment came face to face with Karma.

Modern science has taught us to think in terms of what we once thought incompatibles. Take "matter" for instance. In this atomic age, atoms, the building blocks of matter, are no longer defined as ultimate indivisible particles, but as dynamic systems, best described by mathematical formulae. Their solidity is a myth, because other particles called leptons permeate everything, yet interact with nothing. At this point the distinction between the theologian's spiritual and material substance seems meaningless. However, the dependable laws of atomic behavior are more important than ever. We are learning that the multiplicity and variety of interacting patterns is characteristic of world order—is, indeed, its essential and basic feature.

Perhaps the most startling consequence of the scientific discovery of the DNA code of every living body, which indicates that not substance, but a formula is basic to the existence of each of us, is the new possibility it opens of resurrection. If there is an eternal file for the pattern, as there seems to be, what matters the fate of our restless dust? The tides and mighty trade winds of endless time may sweep it from one temporary lodgement to another, many disperse, may scatter, may reinvolve what was our dust in countless new patterns, but the unique DNA code of each of us, an eternal formula, is apart from all turmoil.

The stoic philosophers were notable among Greek thinkers for giving a distinctly religious and ethical implication to their central doctrine of the orderliness of nature. Zeno of Citum, its founder, whose dates are from 335 to 265 B.C., taught that Divine Reason, the *Logos*, pervaded the universe and kept it in order. Man's ethical obligation, and his spiritual salvation, was to accept nature as an expression of World Reason, or Providence, and to submit serenely, yes happily, to the natural ills as well as the natural good aspects of life. Man himself, he held, in all his comings and goings was determined by Universal Law. His sole freedom was that, through wisdom, he could realize his status and thereby acquire the right mental attitude toward it.

The Confucian concept of *Li* goes even further. *Li* is the principle in the infinitely complex and exquisitely balanced cosmic order, of which the moral order is one of the subordinate yet constituent patterns. Hence, if the balance in appropriate roles between sovereign and subject, or pupil and teacher, or parents and children is upset, it will be reflected in an imbalance in the Milky Way. Rivers may flood their banks, or famine may come, or the cycles of rains may be disturbed. The followers of Confucius considered the universe a mechanism, but it was certainly as delicately interrelated as an organism; one is tempted to think in terms of cosmic psychosomatic responses as one studies Confucianism.

To return to Stoicism and Zeno's teaching, he believed that the universe itself was subject to a cyclical pattern of destruction and renewal. Each complete cycle was, he believed, terminated by a universal conflagration out of which the new cycle was born. After each cycle there was literally a new heaven and a new earth and so on forever. But the "forever" of time we cannot grasp said his fellow philosopher Strato, for time is continuous, and therefore of necessity different from any series of discontinuous data, such as numbers, by which we strive to grasp it. It is meaningless

Pattern

to add a day to eternity. "Forever and a day" we say, and we have said nothing.

It was another Stoic, Cleanthes, who succeeded Zeno as head of the Stoic School, whom St. Paul quoted in his sermon on the Areopagus. He spoke of the altar to an unknown God. The line from Cleanthes' poem was: "For in him, we live and move and have our being," and because St. Paul declared the description applicable to the relationship between a Christian and his God, he, too, stressed the deep and fundamental harmony between man and the orderly universe of which he is a part.

The concept of a cosmic pattern is anything but sporadic and local. The Rig Veda of India celebrates Rita, later known as Dharma, the sacred universal law which determines cosmic, including human, patterns. It determines the lawfulness of moral and religious behavior even while it keeps the stars in their courses. The god Varuna, assisted by Mithras, is the guardian of Rita and tireless spies and informers report to him any human being's deviation from paths of truth and piety. As day follows night, as tides rise and fall, and spring comes after winter, all obedient to Rita, so man must follow justice and eschew wrongdoing or be destroyed.

It is likely that many of us in the twentieth century have glimpsed the majesty of the concept of cosmic order, or universal pattern, not from direct knowledge of ancient writings sacred to various religions, but from Greek tragedy. Sophocles, speaking through the lips of Antigone, in her defiance of King Creon's decree of death for anyone burying her slain brother, spoke of allegiance instead to

> The infallible, unwritten laws of Heaven,
> Not now, or yesterday, they have their being
> But everlastingly and none can tell
> The hour that saw their birth.

Antigone, it is true, was speaking of moral laws, but for many thoughtful Greeks the laws of conduct and the laws of being were inextricably intertwined.

A strange and half-legendary sage was born not in Greece, but in China, in 604 B.C. He wrote a slender volume on "The Way of Life." At the end of his life he rode off alone on a water buffalo into the twilight of the desert. He was Lao Tzu, the founder of Taoism, which in its original form was strangely like Stoicism. Lao Tzu's little treatise was a simple, austere command to discover and follow nature's path, or "Tao," its order, its pattern, its inherent design. Unfortunately, mixed with the simple directness of the message there was much verbal doodling, perhaps a nervous space-filling device on the part of Lao Tzu, perhaps mischievous mystification, for it was sheer nonsense. At any event, it afforded so-called "interpreters" a chance, perhaps malicious, to invent superstitious meanings at odds with the sage's teachings, so that Taoism as we know it is no longer pure.

Witter Bynner's translation of "The Way of Life" is purged of this nonsense, and to read it is a joy. Of the Universe, Lao Tzu says that it is deathless, being infinite, for only the finite and limited knows death. Lao Tzu prefers not to speak of "the Universe." Instead he writes of "Tao," "the path" or "the way." It is something like "the divine pattern" or the *Logos* of the Greeks, beyond reach of the senses and also exceeding thought and imagining. It is the basic mystery. According to Lao Tzu, "Those who know don't say, and those who say don't know." In the *Tao Te Ching* Lao Tzu wrote: "The Tao which can be conceived is not the real Tao." In other words, this ground of all existence is ineffable and transcendent, and man's attitude toward it should be worshipful ecstasy.

In a second sense, however, Tao is imminent in nature, and we are aware of it as a universal and dynamic law or rhythm. It is strangely like Bergson's conception of the *élan vital*. As a creative force Lao Tzu was inclined to think of it as a mother principle, benign and slow, more congenial to man than the later Roman concept of a stern *lex aeterna*. There was also a third or ethical aspect of Tao. Taoism, like Stoicism, concluded that the only proper attitude toward the metaphysical Tao was quietism, or harmony with nature through cheerful acceptance of whatever happens.

The ethical mood of Taoism was in perfect accord with the spirit of the epitaph raised to the memory of Epictetus, a Stoic: "I was Epictetus, a slave, and maimed in body, and a beggar for poverty, and dear to the immortals."

It has been claimed that neither Stoicism nor Taoism are properly classified as religions, being rather practical philosophies of life. However, anyone agreeing with Goethe's statement that the problem of every religion is to reconcile man to the inevitable will not hesitate to consider them religions in the most profound meaning of the word.

There is an aspect of Taoism labelled by Huston Smith "Esoteric Taoism" that has much in common with Zen Buddhism. The worshipper waits with a blank mind, senses dulled, impulses stilled. In this condition, he finally achieves a moment of complete insight, which fills his being with bliss. A student of Gestalt psychology would recognize this as our common experience of "closure." It is the happy moment of relaxation when a puzzle suddenly falls into shape as a pattern.

It is experienced with varying degrees of intensity in daily living, as when a design is finished and we put down the brush or a long overdue letter is written, stamped, and sealed. It is experienced most luminously in thinking, when after the frustration of bewilderment and confusion we suddenly see through the puzzle. We say we "get the hang of it" or that at last we "see our way." After years of intense striving, Buddha, sitting under the bo tree, finally experienced this moment of insight, with its relaxation of tension. From that moment on he knew the "way." He could describe the path to his followers.

The fatalism inherent in Islamic teaching differs in an important way from the concept of universal law, as envisioned by Taoists, Buddhists, or Stoics. For Islam, Fate, *Kismet*, represents the fiat of Allah; Allah, the one god, wills the law. Allah is true and just, good and compassionate, but what he wills is nevertheless arbitrary, not ineluctable. He could will otherwise. Zeus bowed to universal law; Allah creates it.

Of all the ancient gods those most aware of their limited power were the Norse gods who knew the twilight of their doom was woven in the texture of the universe and that they were as powerless to save themselves as to save mankind.

The essence of Islamic religion is unquestioning submission to the will of Allah, an idea natural to peoples nurtured in despotism, but the antithesis of the democratic endeavor to understand and accept essential pattern. The fatalist is driven by a command; the determinist is led by the hope that his understanding of the intricate patterns of being is a factor in their control.

In so far as the Hebrew scriptures portray Jehovah as a person, walking with Adam in the garden in the cool of the evening, making a contract with his chosen people, writing the Ten Commandments on the stone tablets for Moses, the Jewish religion, like Islam, makes the distinction between God and the cosmic pattern, the everlasting order. But it is to the glory of the prophets and psalmists that the infinite conception of the great "I am," again and again, supersedes the finite Creator—God who, moved to anger, sends a flood or, flouted, destroys a neglectful city. In the New Testament in the book of John, it is written that "in the beginning was the word (or Logos) and the word was God," which is an apparent statement of the identity of God with world order.

Youth, today, around the world is growing intolerant of the idea of God. "God is dead!" they shout. Since they have been nurtured in creeds and are almost totally ignorant of the history of religious thought, it is a natural response for them to make.

In his "Commemorative Ode" for the fiftieth reunion of his class at Bowdoin College, Longfellow wrote of the youth of his generation:

> In its sublime audacity of faith
> "Be thou removed" it to the mountain saith
> And with ambitious feet, secure and proud
> Ascends the ladder leaning on a cloud.

The lines apply equally to the "audacity" of the attitudes and actions of the youth of our generation who also have "ambitious" feet, are "secure and proud" (bless them!), but who, being so

Pattern

almost totally ignorant of the past of human thought, "lean their ladder against a cloud," mistaking it for solid support.

That they literally have nothing to support them, their elders cannot tell them, since we no longer speak the same language. If only we could make them see the difference between scientific law and law by fiat and/or custom (which, ironically, is what they think we cannot see); the difference betweeen fact and decree; the chasm between the inviolable and the arbitrary! We rejoice in the spirit of youth that questions and resists inherited prejudice, even while we mourn for the blindness of youth that fails to discriminate between verifiable facts, the patterned relationships of reality, and contrived patterns that are temporary and must be discarded whenever they run counter to those facts.

Perhaps the fault is ours. Perhaps if the older generation were more ready to discard really outmoded ways and ideas, we could save more. Take for instance this idea of God. "God is dead," cry thousands of young people who need to prove both their courage and their freedom, even though with that cry they stamp reverence for humanity as well as for God under foot. If only their elders could have forestalled them saying: "Behold how many gods are dead! Look at the great procession of the gods who have died, beginning with the nature-gods of primitive peoples. See following them in the dimness of the past, mist-shrouded Eneid of the Sumerians; the Egyptian sun-god Ra; nobly conceived Aton; Marduk of proud Babylon, bringer of order out of chaos; Ahura-Mazda, Persian god of light and truth; Greek Zeus, Father of gods and men; Mithras, beloved by Roman warriors; the Numina or "powers" of early Rome, who like Terminus, god of boundaries, became a god only to die; wise Odin, foreseeing his own doom. Yes, gods, hundreds, perhaps thousands of gods are dead, but the idea of deity is not. Deity, transcendent and indefinable, but ever sought, is still man's inmost hope. "It is in justice, in law, in pattern and in order that we glimpse hints of God's majesty."

And it is in the discipline of logic and in linguistic philosophy today, as exemplified in the writings of Wittgenstein who died in 1951, that the necessary truths of ontology are seen as functions of logic. The preoccupation of the beginning of the century with epistemology, the theory of knowledge, has shifted to the study of the validity or the logic of propositions concerning reality that are embedded in tautologies and contradictions. In the philosopher's search for necessary truth, he comes upon fixed patterns such as "A is A" and "A is not not-A." This is the *a priori*, the-given-in-advance, of all probing. It is a pattern of reality. We have met it before as "The Great I Am," as "Om," as "Tao," as "Divinity," as Logos."

The search for ultimate pattern is of necessity endless. This truth, man's searching spirit constantly reaffirms. The pattern of known reality expands. It is endlessly creative. Man cannot make a graven image to represent truly the living mystery of ever-unfolding reality. Yet equally with novelty he comes upon omnipresent order. William Cullen Bryant in his deeply religious poem *To a Water Fowl* responded with a sense of the sublime to the time-space pattern of bird migration. "He who from zone to zone, guides through the boundless sky thy certain flight, in the long way that I must tread alone will lead my steps aright."

Today the rhythm of migration in birds, the punctual predictable runs of the grunion, timed to tides, the homing of pigeons, photoperiodism in plants, the elaboration of Darwin's study of the periodicity of the sleep of plants, all these and other related rhythms are objects of intensive and sophisticated laboratory research undertaken by biologists of world renown. Even nonscientists are fascinated by the disclosure of the "living clocks" of the animate world synchronized with the master clock, the sun; and trained specialists are uncovering the incredible patterning dominating the minutest cells.

Observed data, once seen only as awe-inspiring mysteries beyond all possibility of explanation, are today emerging from laboratory study as the most recently understood, most complex and pervasive and no less awe-inspiring and basic rhythm of life.

The ancient Greek philosophers asked whether reality was one or many. They asked also whether change or permanence is its basic nature. The wisest among them early grasped the primacy of orderly change and the multiplicity inherent in unity.

Pattern

The great religions of our human past have held worshippers most securely when the reality they called divine was recognized as ultimately beyond human knowing. Only the infinite can endure the scrutiny of probing telescope and mircroscope without stop. Chaos, the absence of order, would baffle their scrutiny by rendering it meaningless. But systems beyond systems and orders within orders allure and enchant man to an endless quest, "a boundless task."

CHAPTER VIII
Half Gods

Tamerlane (1333-1419), great mogul conqueror of most of southern and northern Asia, was a demigod. His father was a beam of light from a star; light being one of the acceptable disguises for a god, when he wooed a mortal. Tamerlane, or Timur Leng, Timur-the-lame, took Samarcand for his capitol. The name Samarcand is linked in our ears with the tinkling sound of camel-bells, as laden caravans set forth across the desert on "the golden road to Samarcand."

Tamerlane made Samarcand resplendent above the other cities of central Asia. He adorned it with graceful mosques, with cupolas of turquoise blue. He erected Madras-Sas, or libraries, filled with manuscripts; to them both scholars and students came thronging, drawn by the magnets of the manuscripts. The teaching was free and informal. The students crowded close to the scholars, held only by their eagerness to learn and rewarded for studious attention by their growing competence. Often the scholar expounded a manuscript to a group under an orchard tree, for Tamerlane had made the city fragrant with orchards and garden plots. It was peaceful with the sound of running, splashing water in fountains on the palace grounds.

For his own burial place, Tamerlane built lovely Goor Ameer, a mosque with a pointed, blue-tiled cupola. Fragrant basil perfumed the shrine; doves were permitted to fly in under the lofty dome of the great sanctuary, a cool, uncluttered place for meditation. His tomb within the mosque was adorned with a priceless block of dark green jade, delicately carved in flowing Arabic lettering.

Why was Tamerlane considered semi-divine? History knows him as a cruel, almost inhuman conqueror. He delighted when he had killed so many of his foes that he could erect a sizeable

Half Gods

pyramid of their skulls. But for the people of the plains of the Oxus, and particularly for the citizens of Samarcand, which he enriched and beautified with the spoils of half the civilized world, he was a benefactor, a builder of beauty, a conquering hero, and as such was raised to the status of the semi-divine. Today, in our Western World, colleges would have vied with each other to bestow honorary degrees on him. For his people and his time, the highest honor was to bestow divinity. Instead of a citation, he was granted an appropriate miraculous, if legendary, birth.

In the fourth century, Alexander the Great, conqueror of Persia, as well as most of the known world, spent two years in Samarcand. He, too, was a demigod, but a self-styled one. To reach the climax of oriental splendor in which he learned to live after conquering Persia, Alexander had himself proclaimed "God-King." This presumption displeased the Greek soldiers in the army which had won him world dominion, and one of them, at least, dared tell him so. He paid with his life for the insult to Alexander's "divinity."

Asclepius was a kindly demigod of ancient Greece, venerated for his healing powers. He may have been a man who actually lived about twelve hundred years before Christ who united in his person the roles of healer and priest, a not uncommon combination. Hundreds of temples were dedicated to him in Greece, and many hundreds of miraculous cures were reported for those believers who came to his temples for the healing rite known as "incubation" or "temple sleep." The sick seeking a cure spent the night sleeping in the dormitory or *abaton* connected with the temple, and there they were visited often, as in a vision, by Asclepius or one of his priests who gave advice. In the morning the patient left the temple cured.

There are at Epidaurus many inscriptions recording the cures. They indicate the advice given included instruction about diet, exercise, and baths. Even today in some of the Aegean Islands and in Sicily and southern Italy there are churches where incubation is practiced, and no wonder, for it works. Most patients would follow a doctor's prescription to the letter if they were convinced he was a god. And if one happened to be suffering from a hysterical ailment, the situation is more ideal for suggestion to work than in most miracle-working shrines.

Historians have surmised that considerations of shrewd statecraft instigated the deification of the Roman Caesars, beginning with Caesar Augustus. As the subjugated peoples who composed the vast Roman Empire worshipped many different gods, the Empire lacked a much-needed spiritual unity, which emperor worship could supply. Already in the far-flung, heterogeneous Roman Empire their common fear of the name "Caesar" held the subject states together. Some authorities hold that all religion is founded on fear; undoubtedly, emperor-worship was.

Moreover, Rome showed subtle insight, when it instigated emperor-worship. It endowed it with mystery and gave it a transparent shroud of awe. Men were not asked to believe that the bodily Caesar, living or dead, was a god. But his "genius" was a god, both while Caesar lived and after his death. The genius was a vaguely defined spiritual self, elusive but deathless. In a sense it was a person's replica, in a sense his guardian. It attended him while he lived and like the Egyptian *ka* survived the death of the body. Unlike a pale shade blown about like a withered leaf in the underworld, the genius retained a measure of power in the world of the living.

Augustus Caesar inaugurated the worship with a temple to God-Julius on the Forum, where Julius Caesar's body had been buried. One emperor, Liberius Caesar, tried to protest: "I confess that I am mortal, Conscript Fathers," but another force, namely loyalty to the state, which had been amalgamated with the religious motive, drowned protest. He learned, as unfortunate subjects had already learned, that not to worship the emperor was to disavow allegiance to the state as well. A rebel against the state religion was automatically a traitor.

Superficially similar but possibly different was the recently discarded dogma of the more than human status of the emperors of Japan. As direct descendants of the Sun Goddess their persons were semi-divine. In accordance with the etiquette of State Shinto, Japanese emperors were honored in all their comings and goings with ceremonial ritual which attested to their sacred status. Yet

Half Gods

it was reported that after the formal Japanese surrender to General MacArthur, when it was suggested to the Emperor that he should issue a proclamation renouncing his divinity, he hesitated at first, saying it would be difficult to disclaim what he did not possess. His people, he said, did not consider him a god in the Western sense.

In her book *The Chrysanthemum and the Sword*, the late Ruth Benedict noted that Japan's deification of the emperor was the continuance of a practice long common in the islands of the Pacific. As late as the eighteenth century the person of the island chief was sacred. If he so much as touched a spoon with his teeth when eating, the spoon became holy and taboo. The majesty of his god-status actually imprisoned him in his palace, for since any spot of earth on which his foot rested thereby became holy, only he could own it, and therefore to permit him to wander freely about his island was unthinkable. Similar beliefs hemmed in the Sacred Chief on Tonga and on Samoa and were passed on to Japan to render the Emperor a state prisoner by virtue of his very holiness.

What is the dividing line between ceremony and religious behavior? State Shinto grew up to do reverence to ancestors and in particular to perpetuate the legend of the descent of the Emperor of Japan from the Sun Goddess. The State supported elevenhundred thousand shrines and their attendant Shinto priests. But unlike Buddhism and Christianity, this vast establishment was not regarded as religious. Its priests were forbidden by law to teach any dogma or conduct services of worship. They were masters of ceremonies. In a shrine, a priest could purify a newly elected government official by waving before him a wand from which fluttered hemp and streamers of white paper. With a shrill chant he could summon the gods to partake of food offered, but these were ceremonies. When the Emperor himself appeared before the Shrine on a day of festival to ask a boon from Heaven for his people, the government offices were closed.

A Buddhist or a Christian could take part in a State Shinto ritual and bowing deeply present a twig of the sacred tree with strips of white paper attached to it and according to Japanese ideology would have performed a ceremonial but not a religious act. This interpretation holds also for the traveller who pours lustral water over his hands before stepping over the high sill to enter the beautiful Meiji shrine on the outskirts of Tokyo.

Perhaps so, but it may be that Jung is more nearly right when in his *The Psychology of the Unconscious* he suggests such a ceremony is also deeply religious. "The gods" Jung equates with "libido." Shinto, with its reverence for ancestors, connects through its ceremonious ritual our present living selves with "the root of the whole of humanity." It gives us a glimpse of our own immortality, as we feel ourselves part of the race "which is never extinguished." Each of us, Jung says, is "only a twig broken off and transplanted."

Moreover, as it is possible to consider any ritualistic acts as religious, whether it is building a shrine, making a pilgrimage to a sacred mountain, prostrating oneself toward Mecca, crossing oneself, saying a prayer, or presenting a twig with fluttering white streamers, I find invalid the Emperor's belief that his people did not consider him a god. State Shinto had given him the power of a god. To serve him was the highest value in Japanese life. It was because they accepted him as a god that thousands of Japanese soldiers in the late war hurled themselves without question on death with the emperor's name on their lips—martyrs to their faith.

More to be pitied than any mortals entrapped by divinity are, it seems to me, the "Living Goddesses" of virginity in Nepal. The "Living Goddess" is a child selected at four or five by a committee of Hindu priests. Until her puberty, she is destined to live in royal state, but in seclusion, worshipped but imprisoned. As substitutes for carefree play and a gleeful childhood, she must accept veneration and the decorum becoming a goddess. The curse of heaven stands guard over her perpetual virginity. If any man becomes her husband, the gods, it is held, will punish him with death. It is a modern re-enactment of the life stories of the Vestal Virgins of Imperial Rome, except that in Rome, it was a Vestal Virgin, if she proved no longer virgin, who was buried alive.

Half Gods

Perhaps it is not correct to classify Prince Siddhartha Gautama as a demigod. He himself never claimed to be more than a mortal. Some of his ardent followers consider him completely divine. Others believe that as Lord Buddha he attained divinity. We can add to the historical facts already cited that he was born to King Sudhodanna Gautama and his wife Queen Maya in the small Kingdom of Sakyus at the foot of the Himalaya Mountains, in the plains of the Ganges. His father was overwhelmed with joy, for he was over fifty years old and had no other children. He had prayed to all the Hindu gods for a son to rule after him. At the news of the birth of the young prince, people came from every part of the small kingdom to bring gifts. Among others, were seven holy men from the Himalaya Mountains, who according to legend, when they saw him exclaimed in unison: "Such a beautiful child was never born before!" And then in a second breath exclaimed together: "He will grow up to be a very great man!"

When Prince Siddhartha was twelve, at a great celebration in the royal palace, he put on the sacred thread, spoke the Vow of Allegiance to the Hindu religion and began the study of the sacred books, the Vedas, written in Sanskrit. In them, he learned of the Trimuti, the three-fold nature of Brahma the Creator, who is also Vishnu the Preserver, and Siva the destroyer; he learned also that castes are inherent in creation, that reincarnation is governed by the great law of cause and effect called "Karma" and that Nirvana, reabsorption in the World-Soul, is the reward of superlative excellence.

For four years the young prince was a student and at sixteen, education completed, he married the beautiful Princess Yosodhara. Their fairytale life of happiness together in their luxurious castles, with hunting lodges and game parks, countless servants and all the delights of oriental opulence, lasted for ten years. Then of a sudden in encounters with sickness, poverty, death, and a contented mendicant monk, the young prince, who had just become a father, faced the reality of suffering. As we have already recounted he left everything he had known and loved to become a beggar-monk, seeking to know how everyone, not just the privileged, might be happy. That night when he stole away from the Palace and his wife and sleeping child, has been known for nearly 2500 years as the "Night of Great Renunciation." Prince Siddhartha was then 29.

For seven years he wandered from place to place seeking wisdom. He went to the renowned teaching monks, Adara and Udaka, and they told him to study the Vedas. This he had already done, and the problem of evil and suffering and frustration was as great as ever.

For a time, he associated with five other monks who told him the road to salvation was through self-denial and self-torture. The prince nearly starved himself to death, but came no nearer to the wisdom he sought. So he renounced the ascetic way, but not his search for wisdom. All the world knows how, after weary days and months of wandering from place to place the great moment of enlightenment came to him while he was sitting quietly under the bo tree in deep self-communication. He then saw Karma, the law of life, in a new light; from good must come good, he thought, and from evil, evil. He gave himself the task of extracting the consequences of this central thought—amplifying it and simplifying it into the most adequate ethical map he could make.

The first consequence was a negative one. He concluded that prayers and sacrifices to the many Hindu gods were useless. If Karma, the law of the deed, holds, then the actions of men, not the interference of the gods determine the outcome. Then in a blinding flash, he realized that useless gods are idols. To worship such gods is evil. Then, he reasoned further, the Vedas which say men must pray to the gods and worship them are not sacred books, and the priests, who say they are holy, deceive us. Along with discrediting the Vedas, went also the caste system they sanctified. The Buddha at once taught there are only two kinds of men—good men and bad. Finally, he concluded, Brahma did not create the world. It always was.

This was his sweeping, magnificent break with tradition. His positive doctrine is strangely like Aristotle's, whose near contemporary in time he was. The wise man takes the middle road between extremes if he wishes, as he must, to be happy. He does

Half Gods

not drown himself in pleasures, he does not crucify himself with torments.

He even spelled out in the eight rules of life, how a man could set himself on the Middle Path: Right belief, Right resolve, Right speech, Right behavior, Right occupation, Right effort, Right contemplation, and Right concentration—these will take and keep him there. For his followers he was willing to elaborate further each part of the eight-fold path. For instance, the five commands of uprightness under the heading "behavior" are as explicit and simple as the Ten Commandments. They are: do not kill; do not steal; do not lie; do not commit adultery; and do not get drunk.

Buddha thought of himself as a teacher who had found a great truth which he was constrained to impart. But in the years following his death his followers elevated him to the status of a god. They did not deny his human parentage or his death but did insist that the living Buddha was an incarnation, the supreme incarnation of Brahman.

Considering again Hindu doctrine from which Buddhism is derived, I find myself in disagreement with a recent critical exposition of the Hindu exposition of the Hindu conception of ultimate reality upon which Buddha's teaching rests. Kenneth Rexroth in one of his reviews of the Classics (LXXIII to be exact) in the *Saturday Review of Literature* wrote that the "Geta" often called "The Lord's Song" in the Bhagavad Gita portrays a personal god Ishvara behind Brahman the inscrutable ground of being. He called this Geta of the third century before Christ a manual of devotion to a personal deity. That it may be.

Of the many translations of the original Sanskrit which Mr. Rexroth cited, I have read only the familiar one by Swami Probhavananda and Christopher Isherwood, from which I gather that Ishvara is not a personal creator-god, prior to and necessary for the existence of the infinite, formless, and essentially inscrutable Brahman, but is, like Krishna himself, the narrator, a manifestation of Brahman, just as Buddha is. Through such a manifestation mortals who cannot think cogently in infinite and impersonal terms strive to grasp something of the majesty of infinite being.

Brahman remains the ultimate, formless source of gods and of Maya, the illusory world of existence, which includes the *atman*, each person's individual soul. As the Geta itself states: "Ishvara represents all that the human intellect can know of God; Brahman in the absolute sense cannot possibly be known by the conscious mind."

We must realize that this Hindu concept of ultimate reality as infinite and unknowable was shared by the Greek traveller-poet Xenophanes, who is said to have lived from 570 to 480 B.C. In a didactic philosophical poem he noted the different ideas of gods held by people in different parts of the world and concluded that men could conceive of gods only in their own image. In Thrace, he said, men described the gods as blue-eyed and red-haired just as Thracians were, whereas in Africa men worshipped gods who were black and snub-nosed. They could not grasp the idea of an impersonal god and so clung to gods in their own image.

Xenophanes even anticipated Rupert Brooke's lampoon of a personalized God in Brooke's poem "Heaven." The Greek philosopher declared that if horses and oxen could form ideas of gods, they would undoubtedly portray them as horses and oxen. In Brooke's poem, Heaven, as imagined by fish, would have:

> Wetter water slimier slime!
> And there they trust there swimmeth One
> Who swam ere rivers were begun,
> Immense of fishy form and mind,
> Squamous, omnipotent and kind,
> And under that Almighty Fin
> The littlest fish may enter in.

Recognizing clearly the danger man ran of demeaning the concept of Deity by personalizing and therefore limiting it, Xenophanes adhered firmly to a concept of God very like the Hindu concept of Brahman. He regarded the gods described by Homer and Hesiod as quite as truly a caricature of divinity as we know Brooke's fish deity is.

Half Gods

We know the Buddha had studied the Vedas. He knew at its source the teachings of the Bhagavad Gita regarding the inscrutable divine ground of being. He had put on the green thread of an initiate. When after his enlightenment under the bo-tree, he swept away the countless Hindu Gods, he held fast to two things in Hindu religion that he had been taught but had hitherto not understood. One was the inscrutability of Ultimate Being; the other was the need to hold fast to its manifestation to mankind in Karma—the law of the deed, unswerving, unbending, all-pervading order. His very agonisticism forced him to become one of the world's greatest teachers of the nature of the good life.

After the Buddha died, when his ever-increasing congregations of followers were numbered not by the dozens but by the hundreds of thousands, the Buddha became a god. From India, Buddhism established itself in Nepal, Eastern Turkestan, China, and Japan. It travelled south to Burma, Siam, and Ceylon. It now has its beautiful temples in the Western Hemisphere and in Europe also.

Buddhism is more than the wisdom the Buddha taught of the eight-fold way to happiness by living a virtuous life. It is a religion and for most Buddhists, the Lord Buddha is a god. He is entitled to be called a "half-god" because, although most of his followers admit his human parentage, by his own wisdom and virtue they believe he became divine. His image is worshipped in temples the world over. Prayers are said to him. Flowers are offered to him as he sits on his lotus throne. And legends of his divinity have multiplied through the centuries.

The Mahayana Buddhists, who regard Buddha as a savior, have naturally looked more favorably on these growing legends than the Hinayana or more properly the Theravada Buddhists. Of what sort are these legends? They are of the same substance as the loving myths with which men through the ages have adorned beings they most adored.

During his life, when people impressed by the wisdom and benevolence of the Buddha asked him "Are you a god?" he answered "No"; "An angel?" "No"; "A saint?" still "No." "Then what are you?" He replied, "I am awake." In spite of this, those who felt they loved and honored him most knew he must have been a god.

In strict accordance with the doctrine of reincarnation, the legends taught that before his final reincarnation as the Buddha, he had already been reincarnated in about five hundred and thirty lives. According to the Jatakas, the collection of stories about these lives, he had lived very humble and also most exalted lives, ranging from being as lowly as a frog to being as exalted as a god. He was so pure and so wise that he was fit to merge his being as a Bodista with Brahman in the Nirvana of perfect bliss. But out of pity for men's blindness and consequent misery, he offered himself as a willing sacrifice, even as Jesus did, and foregoing bliss, was born to King Sudhodanna and his Queen Maya as a wondrous babe to live out a long and often painful life of some eighty years. Now in Nirvana— absorbed in bliss and yet still Lord Buddha, a god—he draws all men toward him, not for the sorrows he has known nor a crucifixion as in the case of Jesus, but the strength and beauty of his outstretched jewelled hands.

One of the many legends about his birth was this: his mother Maya, who was 45 at the time of his conception, had a prophetic vision, and while she was carrying him, her side became transparent. When he was born, all nature rejoiced in the event. Trees bent down to make a bower, for his birth came suddenly by a roadside as his mother was journeying to her father's home. His amazing beauty and vigor dumbfounded the attendants. From the first his eyes were wide-open, full, and lustrous. He spoke at once of his own great destiny. There are stories, too, of his temptation by Mara, the Evil One, on the night of his enlightenment. Mara first produced three enticingly beautiful women to woo him into forgetfulness of his quest. Failing to break into Buddha's concentration, Mara then tried to frighten him with threats of violent death by storm and showers of blazing rocks. Finally he engulfed him in absolute darkness. But through the darkness the Buddha was aware of the rocks as flower petals. Finally, the Buddha touched the earth with a fingertip, and the earth responded with a thunderous roar that echoed and reechoed the words, "I bear

Half Gods

you witness." At that Mara and his evil spirits fled.

Not all Buddhists believe these and hundreds of other miraculous legends. Many Buddhists feel the essential duty is to believe in Buddha's Four Noble Truths and read his three Baskets of Wisdom in order to follow the Eight-fold Pathway to Happiness. But there are many who need the addition of mystery, and for them the Enlightened One is Lord Buddha, a god. As the late philosopher Alfred North Whitehead wrote, people need something to stare at. It is obvious that any classification of Buddha as a half-god is open to criticism from two sources, from Mahayana Buddhists, who see in him a very God, and from their opponents, who see in him a leader who is perfected humanity incarnate.

The fact remains that as an object of religious worship, the Buddha-image has both human and divine facets. The underlying assumption necessary for the creation of demi-gods seem to be that when human qualities are raised to the nth degree of perfection, they become divine. This was the Greek formula for their gods, and as we look back upon Zeus and Hera and Athene, with all the awe that clothed them fallen away with the years, they are human, very human, sometimes magnificent, often pitiful—but never gods.

Half-gods, like centaurs, are the creatures of myths. Like Pegasus, half horse, half bird, they tread not earth, but air. But if we take the orthodox view and consider divinity as qualitatively differing from humanity, the alchemy of their mixture produces a demi-god—a Tamerlane or a Buddha—a glamorous warlord overpraised or an incomparable teacher over-adored. Men become demi-gods *honoris causa*. It's a purely honorary title.

CHAPTER IX

Needed: a Devil

In these days of nearly world-wide pessimism about the future of humanity, and scandalized horror at the insistence of rebellious youth, that "God is Dead," few people seem to worry greatly that Satan, or the devil, may also be dead. There seems such abundant evidence that he is very much alive, and busy, that the thought has not occurred to us. Moreover, most of us are so little versed in theology that we, unlike our remote ancestors, have no inkling of the importance of a devil to the continued existence of an omnipotent, omniscient, and benevolent God.

We do know that centuries before the birth of Christ men felt deep concern over the evil they experienced in life and tried to account for it. It seemed to them there must be a source of evil as well as a source of good.

The influential religion founded by Zoroaster in ancient Persia, and still followed by a dwindling but impressive group of about a hundred thousand called Parsee, took the struggle between good and evil as its starting point. The mythology of our Norse fathers was somber with forebodings of the outcome of the same struggle. No one even superficially acquainted with the traditions of the Hebrew religion and of the Christian and Islamic traditions stemming from it can be unaware that Jehovah, God, and Allah, all three, are still engaged in their struggle with the Adversary, Satan. In China and the Orient in general religions influenced by Chinese thought offer instructive insight concerning good and evil.

The Chinese realistically recognize the existence of good and evil as necessary opposites, each implying the other, and taught that neither is experienced in its purity, but always with an admixture of the other. This recognition is part of the age-old philosophy of China. But China escaped the problem of evil, as only

Needed: a Devil

religions based on the postulate that the power which created and now sustains and rules the universe is omnipotent, omniscient, and benevolent create for themselves the "problem" of evil. The problem is how a being, all-powerful, all-wise, and entirely good can permit evil to exist. It is all too evident that it does exist. Polytheism has no grave problem because a multitude of gods, like a multitude of people, have varying degrees of power, wisdom, and benevolence. But like all absolutes, Absolute power, Absolute knowledge, and Absolute goodness found in one deity called "The Absolute" raise difficult problems. The usual solutions for monotheistic religions is to limit the absolute power of God by positing a Satan or Evil Being, equal or nearly equal in power to God, in order to preserve intact the absoluteness of God's wisdom and knowledge and his unflawed goodness. To save God's virtue, Satan must exist.

Chinese philosophy, which uniformly dispenses with a creator-god and begins with "what is," does not need to create a devil to explain evil; yet it can recognize evil as a facet of existence and for the most part is concerned with practical ways of dealing with it. One of China's most profound ideas, central to almost all its great philosophical and religious teaching, is the familiar symbolism of Yang and Yin. The symbol is a circle divided into black and white areas.

The opposites of black and white are equal halves of the whirling circle or wheel. No straight diameter divides the circle, and the black and white segments thrust into each other's area. Moreover, in the white territory there is a small spot of black and in the black an equal area of white. The symbol can show only static opposites, but imagine it a whirling circle and one can picture the tension of counterbalancing forces. Yang and Yin stand for the polarity of all the basic opposites we experience in life: for good opposed to evil, male versus female; for positive versus negative, summer versus winter, hope versus despair, life versus death.

Subtle and germinal philosophical and religious ideas are packed into the concepts of Yang and Yin. Yang, the white, can stand for Heaven as represented in all the positive fructifying forces in the Universe. Hence it is the sun-god, the sunlight, which makes the mother Yin, the dark, cold earth, fruitful.

As early as the third century before Christ there was already a well-organized group known as "Yang-Yin Experts" explaining to less informed people the cosmic importance of these opposites. Yin originally was a Chinese character for a whole cluster of qualities associated with the Chinese symbol that represented the "north side of a hill": coolness, moistness, shadiness, quietness, submissiveness, gentleness, and finally femininity. Yang was the character for the contrary qualities. Neither was intrinsically good or bad to begin with. There were those who liked Yin and coolness and femininity better than Yang with its full sunlight, activity, and masculinity, and vice versa. The tendency to think of Yang and Yin as things instead of qualities, then as agencies, fell in with natural animistic thinking and eventually transformed them into powers. It also hastened the tendency to think of them as good and bad, in opposition.

From the dynamic opposition of Yang and Yin come all the joys and sorrows we experience, come birth and death. From their embrace the seasons issue, and night and day. Day can be identified with Yang, as can life, while night and death can be identified with Yin. Yang and Yin together are *Tao* and Tao is the idea of law, order, or pattern central to all religion.

The Oriental concept of the whirling wheel of Yang and Yin, which is to be found in Confucianism as well as in Zen Buddhism and is central, of course, to Taoism, dispenses with speculation about a creator. It is a symbol of cosmic law, of Tao. As an abstraction, a sketch, a map of what is, an attempt to state the dynamic in static terms, it is bound to be inadequate. It is the footprint left by the vital impulse of cosmic process, when the impulse is suddenly arrested and the vitality gone out of it.

The symbol is no more like felt experience than the stilled blades of an airplane propeller are like the transparent misty circle of haze they present in flight. Yet though as a symbol it cannot be expected to duplicate reality, it does explain the presence and the rôle of evil, without compelling man to create a devil. For the followers of Lao Tzu, for Confucius, and for the Buddha it was

Needed: a Devil

a symbol of "the Way." It was what the *Logos* was for Greek thinkers. It was a symbol of what scientists mean today when they say "Nature."

At a later date than Confucius, Chu-Hsi (1130-1200 A.D.), a neo-Confucianian identified Heaven with *Li*. Li, like Yang, is a dynamic, vivifying principle opposed to inert *Ch'i* as Yang is opposed to Yin. It bears a striking resemblance to Bergson's concept of the *élan vital*, or vital impulse, which eternally generates matter as it meets opposition. Bergson's "revolutionary" concept startled the Western World at the beginning of the twentieth century by its daring novelty. Yet is was an old idea to the Orient.

Confucianism, as thus reshaped by Chu-Hsi, has been the educational nourishment of the Mandarin class in China until recently and produced a religious atmosphere comparable to Greek and Roman stoicism. The accepted doctrine of the soul, following from the concept of Yang and Yin, was that each man has two souls, a heavenly Yang-soul and an earthly Yin-soul. The first is called *shen* and the second, *kwei*. At death the shen soul returned to Yang and the kwei to Yin. The words of the Christian burial service acquaint us with a similar and yet subtly different idea: "Dust to dust and spirit to God who gave it." Somehow, our dust seems more dessicated than kwei is, and not a soul at all. Perhaps because kwei, the Chinese earth-soul, is a very lively sort of dust, this belief opened the way for animistic beliefs that bred a multitude of godlings.

It was easy, perhaps inevitable, that Yang and Yin should be construed in moral terms. Yang became the good, Yin the evil principle, and as everything both animate and inanimate is the result of the union of Yang and Yin, it was a natural next step to speak of things as well as people as having two souls, shen and kwei. It was equally easy to consider one a benevolent and one a malicious soul. Rain, for instance, is both good and bad. It can end a drought. It can start a flood. The end result is a rampant animism with bean-curd gods and gods of boils; everywhere gods to be adored, gods to be propitiated.

In ancient Persia or Iran, the religion of Zoroaster took the problem of evil as its starting point, and the angel Ahura-Mazda, the one god, radiant, luminous—the god of truth and justice—took on himself the struggle against Ahriman—the god of evil, also called Angra Mainyn.

Zoroaster or Zarathustra, the founder of Zoroastrianism, was born in Persia somewhere between the Tigris and the Oxus rivers in the seventh century before Christ, or possibly even earlier. There is some doubt about the authenticity of the commonly accepted facts of his life, which have been generously embellished with legend. It is probably true that he was farm-born and reared, the third child in a family of five children. There is proof that his wife's name was Hvon and that she probably brought him an acceptable dowry, for Hvon means "having fine oxen." The marriage must have lasted some years, for they had four children. After Hvon's death, Zoroaster married a second time, and two children were born of this marriage. By the time Zoroaster took a third wife, legend had begun to weave its magic tales about him. His third wife by whom he had no children is now, in our century, his Celestial Spouse from whom in Heaven's good time three children are to be born. Two will be puissant prophets, and one will be a Messiah. The legends adorning his birth and infancy are unusually colorful and splendid. Fully 3,000 years before he was born, startled seers caught a vision of him, majestic and commanding in the sky; and as his advent drew nearer, a mere three centuries away, an ox, gifted with human speech, testified to his coming and to his message. As the time of his conception drew near, the demons, whom he was so valiantly to oppose, exerted their not inconsiderable power to prevent his conception, which however in the end they could not circumvent. At his birth, all nature rejoiced with angelic songs and fragrant airs, but most clear sign of all, the house where he was born was bathed in a splendor of light, as the child came laughing into the world.

When he was still young, perhaps only fifteen, he began his wanderings through Persia and into India and even China, without money, friends, guide, or comfort. For fifteen years, like other great prophets, he was schooled by the stern teachers of suffering, hunger and loneliness into sure confidence of his message for mankind. He had the dreamer's capacity for visions, and in the midst

Needed: a Devil

of hardship and rebuffs was sustained by a series of mystic audiences with Ahura-Mazda and his attendant angels. Prior to his going for the first time into the presence of Ahura-Mazda, we are told that the Archangel Good Thought instructed him how to enter into the divine presence. He had to step out of his body as out of an unworthy garment and humbly follow Archangel Good Thought into the divine presence of the God of Creation.

Only repeated visions of his god sustained Zoroaster during the ten fruitless years while he struggled vainly to gain adherents for Ahura-Mazda, now often called Ormazd, but still, as always, the god of light and truth, the one God. Zoroaster was acutely aware of the machinations of devils who thwarted and tempted him. They were the servants of Ahriman, God-of-the-lie, twin in time and power to Ahura-Mazda.

Zoroaster's special enlightenment was that life is a continual struggle between good and evil, right and wrong, justice and injustice. His moral and religious message was that man must throw all his weight on the side of the angels. The powers are equally matched, and Ahura-Mazda needs man's help. The warfare is unending. The God-of-the-lie, the principle of evil, is immortal even as is Ahura-Mazda, the God of righteousness, but with man's help he can be held in check.

In a sense this concept of Ahura-Mazda in an eternal struggle with Ahriman, God of negation and evil, is like the Hebrew conception of Jehovah, the God of righteousness, struggling against Satan, Prince of darkness and evil. Yet there is a difference. Moses and other prophets promised the protection of Jehovah for those loyal to him as well as heavenly rewards. Zoroaster called on those who loved righteousness and light to enlist on the side of Ahura-Mazda precisely because he was hard pressed. There was not even a promise of ultimate victory. Just as in the whirling circle of Taoism in which Yang and Yin are in writhing tension, so in Zoroastrianism good and evil are twins. They are equal in power and one implies the other. Life on earth is the eternal strife of good with evil. The struggle is genuine, the outcome uncertain.

But in the life after death the followers of Ahura-Mazda were confident of reward. The followers of the Lord-of-the lie, it was believed, fell into a hell which no religion has painted with more vivid horror. At death each soul had to step upon the Bridge of the Separator over which the soul on the side of righteousness proceeded to the House of Song, while the evil soul fell into torment.

The worship of Ahura-Mazda, established with difficulty, was sustained with difficulty. He yielded gradually not to Ahriman, but to Mithras, like himself a god of righteousness, who could be conceived as a person and not, as was the case with Ahura-Mazda, as a cluster of all the highest virtues.

In the religion of Islam instigated by Mohammed, Allah, the one god, is highly personalized as is Satan, his adversary. The struggle between them shows no signs of abatement to this day. As it is easier to love and serve a person than an abstract idea, the religion of Islam, glorifying Allah, has had great and continued appeal.

Mohammed, the untutored camel driver, who if legend is correct could not sign his own name on that momentous day when the Angel Gabriel first spoke to him, could not be expected to grasp religious ideas except in personal or specific terms. It may be partly because Allah, with his ninety-nine names, and Satan, ever on the alert to thwart Allah's plans, are so firmly established as personalities that Islam won so many converts so rapidly.

The impressive "Verse of the Throne" inscribed in many mosques comes from Sura II of the Koran and has been translated thus: "God, there is no god but he, the living, the self-subsistent. Slumber takes him not, nor sleep. His is what is in the heavens and what is in the earth. . . . His throne extends over the heavens and the earth, and it tires him not to guard them both for he is high and grand."

This is a god, indeed, pictured not only as a person but as a King. He is not an absolute idea; he is an absolute monarch. He is not a composite of values like Ahura-Mazda, he is a Being who can be described by his names, his many names: the merciful, the compassionate, and so on. It is close to the Hebrew and Christian conception of God as a father, a benign and powerful personality.

No one could deny to Mohammed the status of a prophet. He

Needed: a Devil

brought to his fellow Arabs, bewildered and harassed by belief in many petty gods, the doctrine of Allah, the one God, exalted and majestic. To worship him entailed submission to a moral code far loftier and more exacting, far more just and humane, than the prevailing moral code of Mecca, where Mohammed strove, at first vainly, for converts.

Islam means "I submit," and thus to believe in Allah, to be a "true believer," was a matter of allegiance to him in word, thought, and deed. The deeds were minutely and simply spelled out in the Koran. They included both ritualistic and practical behavior, from the manner, the place, and the times of praying to the giving of alms, kindness to animals, and the tolerance that recognizes all men as brothers.

Islam (alas for tolerance!) was also imbued with missionary zeal coupled with military might. It inspired such fanatic loyalty to Allah, the one true God, that an infidel, an unbeliever in Allah, became automatically a servant of Satan. As Jews and Christians were equally convinced, for their part, that loyalty to Allah was disservice to God and therefore service to Satan, the stage was set for a holy war. The old struggle of good against evil, of God against the Devil, of light against darkness played itself out in the maimed and bleeding bodies of men loyal to rival gods, mistaking each other for devils and slaughtering each other to serve righteousness. The hatred engendered by men loyal respectively to Allah and to God or Jehovah still menaces the world and clouds the atmosphere in which at the United Nations men of good will strive for peace.

Once a city such as Jerusalem becomes enshrined as sacred to three different religions at once, it becomes a deadly focal point from which the cancer of hatred spreads. Religious loyalties are tenacious even whey they are no more than free-floating slogans, air-borne and sustained like mistletoe by air roots, but let them attach themselves to a definite place, such as a tomb, a shrine, a whole city, then indeed, they are hard to eradicate. They are the sacred causes for which men die.

Norse mythology presents yet another picture of the problem of evil. The Norsemen of old saw existence as a recurrent tragedy ending in the total destruction of both contenders. The good gods, Odin, Thor, and their company, at the horrible conflict of Ragnarök, or Doomsday, would destroy Loki and the monsters of evil such as the Fenris-wolf, but were in turn doomed to be destroyed by them; and mankind, too, was doomed to perish in the conflagration started by Surt from Muspelheim.

The Norse creation myth formed the somber background for the struggle between good and evil. Originally, Ginnungagap, the gaping abyss, existed "everywhere." But not quite everywhere, for it was bounded on the south by Muspelheim, a realm of fire, and on the north by Nifheim, a realm of cold and fog. Sparks from the south and ice from the North came floating into the gaping abyss "which existed everywhere." From the contact of the sparks of fire and the ice a giant, Ymir, was born. He was slain by Odin and his brothers, and his dead body was thrown into the midst of the abyss. His eyebrows became Midgard, the earth, which was joined to heaven by the rainbow, the bridge of the gods.

Niflhel, the realm of the dead, presided over by the hideous goddess Hel, was below the earth. It was surrounded by a formidable wall and the swift and angry river Slid, which ran over a bed of swords. The realm was approached by a bridge guarded by the implacable warrior maiden Modgud. Only those who died of illness or old age were thought to go to the wretched and dismal realm of Niflhel. This fact, incidentally, throws into cruel relief old Scandinavian attitudes toward illness and old age. All the warriors slain in battle and chosen for their courage could mount to Asgard and the realm of Gladsheim, home of the gods, to dine in the great banquet hall of Valhalla with Odin himself.

It was not Odin, King of the Gods, nor even Thor with his mighty hammer who finally killed the Fenris-wolf, the personification of all evil. When the wolf finally gnawed through his chain to devour alike both men and gods, the hero who slew him was Tyr, or Tui, for whom our Tuesdays are named. He was probably none other than Dyans, the old Aryan sky-god strayed into the Norse heaven. It was appropriate that a sky god, a god of light, should slay a wolf of darkness whom the gods had vainly chained. The chain was forged of magic things: the beards of women, the roots of mountains, the sound of the footfalls of cats, the sinews of bears, the spittle of birds, and the breath of fish; and Fenris gnawed at it through the long twilight of the gods, until strand by strand it fell apart.

The Fenris-wolf was killed, but not before he killed Odin. Thor slew the Midgardsorm, the great serpent that coiled about the earth, but Thor fell dead himself from the poison the monster breathed upon him.

No other religion has painted the outcome of the war between good and evil in gloomier colors than the ancient religion of the Norsemen. The winter darkness and cold of their fjords, into whose depth the sun does not shine during so many months of the year, seems to have thrust into their inmost imaginings even as it gripped Ibsen in his portrayal of Brand. Brand, speaking of himself said:

> You children of the southern land
> Were fashioned of another clay
> Than I, born by a rocky strand
> In shadow of a barren brae.

At the close of the play Ibsen, as if translating ancient Norse myth into contemporary drama, has a crushing avalanche bury Brand, champion of a larger, more luminous faith, raised like a banner against the narrow dim religiosity of his co-worshippers. Once again, truth does not prevail, but is crushed.

In the old Norse legend of the war between good and evil, the losing battle for good was fought and lost not once but in cycles of eternal recurrence.

Indeed, all the gods and all mankind, as well as all the cruel monsters, children of Loki, evil incarnate, were slain. Then the conflagration, ignited by Surt's flaming sword, destroyed the world by flame. Presently, out of the ashes, the cycle began again. Even Balder returned, once more to be slain. Again the Fenris-wolf was chained, but chained in vain.

It was long, long ago that some unknown voice called out from the Island of Paxis to a passing Egyptian sailor that "Great

Pan is dead." Well! So are Odin and Thor. So is Ahura-Mazda. But certain problems remain. And they will remain unless by better understanding of the nature of deity, they suddenly become pseudo-problems. One of these is the problem of evil. That will not eliminate evil—far from it—but it will make more plausible the symbol of Yang and Yin.

We have yet to learn that absolutes such as "absolute power" and "absolute goodness" are meaningless concepts because they are inherently contradictory. Think only of the old puzzle: Could God create a rock so huge he could not move it? The greatest possible power or the greatest possible goodness or even ideal goodness we can think. But absolutes are as unthinkable as round squares.

The absolute goodness of God should not have been an idea with the power to drive the members of Jonathan Edwards' congregation to commit suicide out of despair with the comparison of their own qualified and limited goodness, but it did, as the best of them seemed helpless "sinners in the hands of an angry God." If only Jonathan Edwards could have known the wisdom of Lewis Carroll's "Hunting of the Snark." If only he could have grasped the relativity of all values and known that absolute values, "Snarks," when relentlessly hunted down turn out to be "Boojums," mere words!

CHAPTER X

Gadgets, Gestures and the Calendar

Often in Buddhist countries one glimpses prayer-flags fluttering from the tops of poles near shrines and temples. They are more than mechanical signals to catch the attention of a god, as a waving kerchief might arrest the wandering gaze of a friend. They are more, too, than magic gadgets whose every ripple benefits the one who raised it aloft. There is something in a wind-tossed banner that creates a mood. The very stance that must accompany the upward gaze—chin up, chest thrown forward—strangely exalts the spirit.

It is a proud sight to look up from the deck of a ship to the flag of one's own country flying from the mast. A glimpse of it in foreign harbors can easily move one to tears. A king's standard floating from his castle's tower to proclaim the royal presence stirs one by bringing the majesty of power close, even as a prayer-flag brings one in sight of the battlements of heaven.

One can regard only as sheer magic the use of cylindrical boxes stuffed with prayers and passages from sacred texts such as pious Tibetan Buddhists were wont to twirl in the temples of the Dalai Lama until so very recently. Each twirl was a prayer, registered with Buddha. Even more patently magical are the convenient prayer-wheels hanging in countless Oriental temples, waiting for the hands of tourists to spin them and thereby launch a prayer. For the most part, the attitude of travellers, who gladly pay a small fee to spin a wheel, is like their attitude toward the printed fortune in a crisp, sweet Chinese cake; they respect its magic to the extent they feel it just might work.

Obviously, not all prayers are magic, although prayers of strict petition are likely to be. Where the traveller to Benares finds the walk beside the great Hindu temple wet with Ganges water poured in prayerful libation over stone lingams, he is witness to prayer as magic. Such libation is the devout Hindu wife's petition for a son and is a prime example of sympathetic magic raised to the status of prayer. The Hindu woman doubtless remains more conscious of her libation as a prayer than we do when we employ a similar fertility ritual and shower a newly married pair with rice. The magic that was a prayer has become for us a prank, a rather malicious one at that.

St. Augustine, much esteemed among the revered church fathers, warned Christians against the use of prayers of petition. He said the object of prayer was most certainly not to instruct God nor to beg him to change his mind. True prayer was to make the petitioner desire what God desires. One thinks, at once, of that prayer of agony and submission in the Garden of Gethsemane: "Yet not my will but thine be done." In that prayer there was no magic.

It is the opinion of many theologians that prayer implies a belief in a personal god or gods. They hold, too, that it implies a friendly deity, although one who may have been offended and who needs to be appeased. Certainly, one can site instances of vast numbers of such prayers from Judaism, Christianity, Islam, and Zoroastrianism; but we have inherited prayers from religions with no belief in a personal god, from Stoicism, for example, and from Buddhism. I like in particular a quaint and moving Buddhist prayer that holds in loving concern all living things from oak trees and sponges to elephants and microbes—with man included. It reads: "May every living thing, moveable or immoveable, tall, big, or medium sized, clumsy or refined, visible or invisible, near or far, already born or aspiring to birth—may all beings have a happy heart."

Lord Buddha taught that "to have a happy heart" one must be enlightened about the laws of existence and acquiesce in them. This too was a statement of submission, a "Thy will be done"; but the will was universal law, not a personal god's wish.

Votive candles combine sacrifice with prayer, for they are

Gadgets, Gestures and the Calendar

burnt offerings—better still, shining examples of the sacrificial mood at the heart of religion. William James defined true religion as the gift of the best we have to the highest we know.

That best includes ourselves with all our hopes, our fears, our aspirations, so that a man at his devotions is offering himself in allegiance to the highest value he can envision. His votive candle may be a symbol of a dedication too deep to be put into words, to a value beyond clear definition, or it may be debased coinage offered to heaven, a magic *quid pro quo.*

A vow is not a prayer. It is actually the record of a bargain, an arrangement between a person and a celestial power that the person in question will perform certain deeds or give certain gifts if the god in turn will do him a favor. There was in ancient Rome a bureau for the registration of vows; and, let me add, there were severe legal penalties for breaking a vow. Greece, too, regarded vows as legally binding; and in Poseidon's temple, for instance, sailors hung the votive offerings promised to Poseidon if he would save them from shipwreck. In a sense, making a vow was, and is, a type of celestial lobbying rather than a religious rite.

The smoke of the candle, often fragrant with incense, floats upward, as does the smoke of sacrifice from an altar or the charred fragments of a written prayer, wind-blown to waft the message more speedily heavenward. Also carried upward, to assail the gates of Heaven, are the rising rhythms of chanted liturgies. They rise from many ancient churches such as the one adjacent to the monastery on the island of Valamo in Lake Ladoga, where from the day of its founding, black-gowned, black-bearded monks have kept an unceasing chant echoing against its icon-hung walls. The chant ascended without pause like the constantly replenished flame of votive candles. As one group of monks completed the period of their allotted chanting, day in, day out, month after month, year after year, without pause, other monks with deep-throated, unwearied voices picked up the phase just ending and took the places of their brothers now slowly disappearing through the arch of a vaulted passage. Even after the retiring monks disappeared, their chanting formed a faint background for the swelling chords now filling the sanctuary. Surely, such unbroken chanting must send tides of song down the golden corridors of heaven!

People old enough and old-fashioned enough to enjoy Longfellow know his poem about Sandalphon, the angel of prayer. The poet said he owed the legend to the Talmud, which pictures Sandalphon as standing erect at the outermost gate of the City Celestial.

> And he gathers the prayers as he stands,
> And they change into flowers in his hands,
> Into garlands of purple and red:
> And beneath the great arch of the portal,
> Through the streets of the City Immortal,
> Is wafted the fragrance they shed.

Rosaries, as aids to devotion, probably originated in India as thirty-two knots in a string. Each knot stood for an item to be mentioned in a long prayer to Siva. In the Jain rosary a decorative note entered, even as their temples grew lavish with ornamentation. Beads appeared of different colors and as of today the beads could be made of different materials. In Hindu rosaries when the devout encounter a pearl bead, as bead after bead slips through the fingers, they know they must direct thoughts toward Brahma—whom Emerson called "The Over-Soul"—while a coral bead indicates that a prayer is to be directed to a goddess. One must hold firmly to a bead made of human bone when one is praying to Vajrabhairava, who has on occasion slain the god of Death himself. Beads in Sikh rosaries are sometimes of iron, and some Moslem doctrine indicates that the larger the beads the more efficacious they are. Some Moslem rosaries have as many as one thousand beads, each as much as three centimeters in diameter. It is probable that the use of rosaries was introduced into Christianity from Islamic worship and, fortunate for nuns, that the dogma of the number and size of the beads was dropped by the way. Of course, the usual rosaries a Moslem uses have only 99 beads, corresponding to the number of mystic names of

Allah. The Buddhists' rosaries normally have one hundred and eight.

A tourist entering the courtyard of a Chinese Buddhist temple in Bangkok finds vendors of religious merchandise who press upon him pink rice cakes the size and thickness of fluffy pancakes. These the tourist is expected to place as offerings on the low table before the gilded lotus-seated Buddha. In order to win merit in heaven by kindness to animals, he is expected also to buy and set free one or more of the pathetic birds in tiny wooden cages, snared on purpose for the temple trade. This presents a nice dilemma—should the tourist take pity on the birds languishing without food or water in their cramped cages, or should he consider the larger problem and refuse to encourage the nefarious snaring of larks and linnets for profit? Perhaps if he stands in immediate need of divine help, he should buy them all on the spot and release them to fly upward with their paeans reaching heaven.

Encyclopedias and dictionaries distinguish between prayers and incantations. An incantation or "spell" is the expression of a wish. If it is a wish for someone's good, it is a blessing; if a wish for evil to befall him, it is a curse. The gracious Mizpah: "The Lord watch between me and thee when we are absent one from another" is commonly considered a blessing. Yet it was not used as a blessing, when first mentioned in Genesis, at a meeting between Laban and his son-in-law Jacob. It was the seal of a bargain, a witness to covenant made visible by a heap of stones that Jacob gathered and over which he swore an oath. If he broke his promise to Laban, God, who would know of his default, was to punish him; and the Mizpah was a conditional curse to recoil on the maker, if he broke faith.

When the Jesuit Fathers painted the eye of God on the ceilings of California missions, they were using a similar technique. The all-seeing eye was watching all the lapses of the wriggling Indian children, Catholic outside but all Indian inside, when the priest was absent or his back was turned. The all-seeing eye was not looking down in blessing. It was on police duty.

Conjuration, also, is not prayer. It occurs when someone with spiritual authority causes evil and/or hostile spiritual beings either to appear in the open or to depart. It has been the professional occupation of medicine men in all primitive religion. Even today in certain Buddhist temples, priests will undertake the cure of psychotic illnesses by a combination of incantation and the pain caused by sharp instruments applied to the scalp to drive out an evil spirit possessing a patient's body.

St. Matthew gives the account of the conjuration by which Jesus drove the devils from two men in a manic state. At his command, the devils fled from their human victims, after protest, and possessed instead a herd of swine, which straightway rushed down a steep incline into the sea and drowned.

Simple, individual, primitive prayers such as children are taught to say before the good-night kiss and the turning off of the light are carried on like social intercourse. They ask Deity to avert danger and bestow blessing: "Keep me safe 'til morning light," and "Bless Papa and Mama and Baby Sister and Fido." Many people never outgrow this simple petitionary form of prayer and in their maturity resort to prayer when in dire need. They seldom or never pray otherwise. They would be astonished to learn that according to Origen, a revered church father, to pray for earthly things is disobedience to God and that Thomas Aquinas agreed that true prayer could not seek to change the course of events. Prayer, he said, should only awaken man's trust in God and enable him to contemplate God's love.

In many religions, prayer is obligatory, at stated intervals. The command in Deuteronomy (6:4 *ff.*) is in essence obligatory prayer: "Hear O Israel, the Lord our God is one Lord, and thou shalt love the Lord thy God with all thy heart, and with all thy soul and with all thy might." This intense preoccupation with the love of God, necessary to the sense of mystical union with him and basic to many religions, helps us to understand what his biographer wrote of St. Thomas, that he cannot have been said so much to have prayed "as to have turned into prayer."

But the obligatory prayer, like the Islamic "salat" performed five times daily after the call to prayer from the minaret, now in our efficient age conveniently recorded and mechanically broad-

Gadgets, Gestures and the Calendar

cast, may be not a mystical experience of rapturous love but a magic rite with distinctly pragmatic value.

I watched a Moslem spread his prayer rug in a crowded railway station in Algiers and prostrate himself toward Mecca with appropriate gestures the allotted number of times, and I did not know whether to think: "How devout he is," or "What a shrewd businessman he is." Was he adoring Allah or was he keeping his accounts straight with Heaven? The question is equally applicable to Christians at prayer. Were they bowing their heads or kneeling to conform with the responses of those about them, or did they really lift up their hearts when, admonished to do so, they replied: "We lift them up unto the Lord."

The customary bodily attitudes in prayer are as varied as the deities to whom the prayers are addressed. We know the ancient Greek stood upright and faced his god expectantly with outstretched arms and open eyes. Most Christians kneel with bowed heads and closed eyes for the mystic encounter, although some omit the kneeling, and still others dance convulsively in the aisles. The devout Moslem prostrates himself seven times toward Mecca. A Moslem's fixed correct procedure when praying is as in many other religions. First he must wash himself. This rite of ablution significantly links religious acts with medical practice, although the pollution the physician washes away before practising his art is material and not spiritual. Then the Moslem spreads his prayer rug before him; at first he stands erect with open hands raised to either side of his face, thumbs just touching the lobes of his ears, even as a surgeon holds his well-scrubbed hands carefully out of the way of contaminating contact, so the Moslem stands as he begins his prayer with the words, "Allahu Akbar." Of course, he faces Mecca and the Kasba, the Holy House, with the sacred Black Stone, a fetish polished smooth by the lips of devout pilgrims.

A Moslem's attitudes in prayer have the graceful sequences of a grave and solemn dance. He must be still standing as he repeats the first surah of the Koran, followed by other passages if he wishes; then bowing from his hips and with his hands on his knees, he extols the perfection of Allah. Like a dancer he returns to the upright position, from which he sinks gracefully to his knees until he can place his hands and his face upon the prayer rug. This cycle from the upright position to the prostration is repeated slowly, usually seven times, with recitation of the creed and prayers and exclamations of devotion and gratitude interspersed.

A Moslem prayer, as quoted by Huston Smith in *The Religions of Man* (Harper and Bros., Publishers, 1958), might be used by a man of almost any faith with little or no alteration. It is as follows:

> Thanks be to my Lord; He the Adorable, and only to be adored. My Lord, the Eternal, the Ever Existing, the Cherisher, the True Sovereign, whose mercy and might overshadow the universe, the regulator of the World, andd Light of the Creation. His is our worship; to Him belongs all worship; He existed before all things, and will exist after all that is living has ceased. Thou art the Adored, my Lord; Thou art the Master, the loving and Forgiving. . . . O my Lord, Thou art the Helper of the afflicted, the Reliever of all distress, the Consoler of the broken-hearted. Thou art present everywhere to help thy servants—O my Lord, Thou art the Creator, I am only created; Thou art my Sovereign, I am only thy servant; Thou art the Helper, I am the beseecher; Thou art the Forgiver, I am the sinner; Thou, my Lord, art the Merciful, All-Knowing, All-loving.

I have seen Jains and Buddhists sitting on their heels with hands palm to palm before an image of Mahavira or Buddha. In Thailand at the shrine of the Emerald Buddha, my friends seated in prayer touched their foreheads to the floor.

The sign of the cross, which the Catholic makes before or after certain acts such as saying grace, the position of a priest's fingers when he raises his hand in blessing, the manner in which he raises the host before his congregation, all are stylized, unvarying fragments of a larger solemn dance, carrying the burden of a

Gadgets, Gestures and the Calendar

prayer. Like rain dances or war dances of primitive people, they are petitionary.

When joy is very great, song alone cannot sustain the emotion. Then one dances for joy as a child does or as King David danced before the Lord, clad only in a linen ephod, when the ark was returned safely to his royal city. Travellers fortunate enough to journey on adventurous voyages on Brazilian rivers may chance to see Caraja Indian girls, also in loincloths, but with geometrical patterns, ancient and traditional, painted on their rich brown skins, dancing for joy and in supplication before their gods. One does not need to travel so dangerously or so far to watch the Southwest Indians of New Mexico in their intricate rain-dance. Their beautiful dance of supplication is danced today as it was danced centuries ago in a past so dim it is properly spoken of as "time out of mind."

Some restrictions on prayer are baffling, such as the old restriction on Jews that they were not to pray publicly when fewer than ten were present. Was it a precaution of safety against hostile Gentiles who might attack them? Or a quorum of propriety to reassure a jealous God of a proper proportion of worshippers? Or a pragmatic prohibition on the part of crafty theologians to keep a few "leftists" from catching Heaven's ear first?

Nothing pertaining to a religion shapes the people under its sway more subtly and more permanently than the regular repetition of sacred rites. The daily, weekly, monthly, yearly recurrence of the intervals of prayer, of fastings or of feastings, of days of contrition and days of rejoicing, etch themselves ineradicably into the pattern of a person's and a people's life. Likewise, the once-in-a-lifetime supreme effort, such as a pilgrimage on foot or camel across the desert to Mecca to kiss the Kaaba and become a hadji, may by the intensity of its continuing effort and resultant status fashion character as effectively as the command that prayer must be offered five times daily.

Hinduism, probably the most long-lived to date of all world religions, does not depend on missionary zeal nor yet on the sword for its perpetuation. Its vigor depends greatly on the subtle and manifold ways religious observances are interwoven with the daily lives of its followers, as well as its ability to absorb differences. Rebels like the Jain leader Mahavira and Buddha, the iconoclast, are elevated to the status of founders of new sects. Journeys to cities which have shrines become pilgrimages. A gift in loving remembrance of a beloved parent becomes more even than ancestor worship. It becomes a symbol of racial piety. By fasts and by feasts the daily routine of life is welded to religion.

Among the most important festivals are Shravani at which time affectionate relationships between brothers and sisters are lifted by symbolic acts to ritualistic status. Dashera, in the early autumn marking the end of the rainy season, is a festival of joy for difficulties overcome, a devout thanksgiving. Following Dashera is the festival of lambs called Diwali. Lakshmi, goddess of prosperity, is honored by this festival. The relationship is held to be close between the glittering brilliance of Lakshmi's worship and the economic prosperity attending enterprises begun at this time. In religious history it celebrates the victory of the demi-god Rama, revered and beloved, over Ravana—an allegory of good over evil. Holi, the most joyous and colorful of all festivals of the year, marks the beginning of spring and unites people in an awareness of a common bond in Hinduism in spite of differences in sects.

In Moslem countries some hundreds of thousands of devout Moslems yearly perform the arduous hadj, circle the black stone the prescribed number of times, sleep where they are supposed to sleep, throw rocks in ritualistic protest at certain other rocks, and proudly thereafter sport a red beard and wear green sashes around their fezzes, signs they have earned their passage to a verdant Paradise. Yet even more influential than this supreme effort, which is a guaranty of Paradise, is the Moslem's daily telling of his beads. Just as water falling drop by drop through the years hollows out a pool for itself in stone, so a lifetime of the daily repetition of the ninety and nine names of Allah fashions a pool of memory and unconscious habit in a man.

The fast of Ramadan, which occurs in the ninth month of the Mohammedan year, unites all Islam in a sense of spiritual superi-

Gadgets, Gestures and the Calendar

ority. From sunrise to sunset during that period, no food and no drink passes the lips of the devout Moslem physically able to discipline himself so strictly. Such self-sacrifice as being really hungry and thirsty each day for a month, for the sake of his religion, raises anyone's self-esteem. It is felt proof of superiority to others who do not put spiritual above bodily values. Over-fearful man, since he first believed in angry gods, has tried to appease them by dog-like cowering. Asceticism and self-denial or self-torture have made him miserable enough to think himself safe. Thus, the observance of Ramadan unites all Islam in a yearly piety of suffering-devotion which literally goes to the marrow of each one. Similarly, many Christians, giving up a pet indulgence "for Lent" consider themselves saintly, although close associates who have had to cope with their Lenten ill-humor are the ones deserving halos.

With wrist-watches almost as universal articles of apparel as shoes and electric clocks in rooms around the world, we forget how intimately the telling of time was once bound up with religious observance. And to know the time, the exact time, is one way of keeping one's finger on the pulse of life. From minarets at punctual intervals the Muezzin's call to prayer and from lofty belfries chimes of bells could and have served in the past, to weave into a common pattern the affairs of heaven and earth. The echoing gongs in Asian temples were no less effective. Even today, in an age grown time-conscious, with watches and clocks reminding us at every turn of life's swift pace, and factory whistles and noonday sirens shattering peace, such sounds from religious edifices still work their magic integration.

No religion has a more impressive calendar of daily observance and of festival and holy days than the Jewish. Historians of the Jews have sometimes overlooked the powerful patterning effect of the Jewish religious calendar. They have tended to consider it miraculous that a religious group so persecuted and so scattered, with so many ethnic strains, could keep its integrity.

However, the calendar, beginning with the weekly observance of the Sabbath in their homes, has built habits and attitudes as deeply founded as life itself. Feast days and solemn fast days have kept the crises of their historic past as much alive for each Jewish child as his own birthday. Moses is as contemporary and as real as current baseball heroes. Each year a child relives the Exodus. Each year, too, he relives the solemn moment when God gave Moses, his Moses, the sacred book of laws called the Torah. His history, for a Jew, is not something written in a book. It is something he reenacts year after swift year in the religious calendar.

To begin with, the observance of the Jewish Sabbath is a happy event, helping to build the family solidarity the world wonders at and so greatly admires. The Sabbath begins at sunset on Friday, when candles are lighted in Jewish homes and the family gathers around the dining table for a special meal, comparable to the old-time Sunday dinner of their Christian neighbors. Attendance at the synagogue, interspersed with rest and pleasurable activities, is the Saturday routine of the Sabbath, which ends as night falls and the family draws together once more as a unit to greet the beginning of a week of work.

The Jewish New Year, coming in September or October, depending on the moon, matches in its solemn mood the rasping, imperious call of the ram's horn, the shofar, that ushers it in. It is called *Rosh Hashanah* and is a time of yearly judgment when God closes his account books for the year just ended and programs the year ahead. No time of the year is so gravely important as are the ten days of Rosh Hashanah ending with Yom Kippur, for during those ten days of grace, there is still time, if one is sincere enough, urgent enough, and fully resolved to do better, to change one's heavenly reckoning from red to black. Yom Kippur, literally the last chance for the year, is a grave and solemn day. During its twenty-four hours, devout Jews neither eat nor drink. Each tries to attend the service in the synagogue before the ram's horn is blown again at day's end to signify that what's done is now done. It is strangely different from the abandon and wild hilarity with which non-Jews normally greet the New Year.

Succos or the Feast of Tabernacles is the Jewish Thanksgiving, a harvest festival. Yet only on the surface is it a day of thanks

Gadgets, Gestures and the Calendar

for the abundant harvest of the year. It has its roots deep in the historic past of the Jews as a people. It is to celebrate freedom by reminding them of their exodus from their slavery in Egypt. On their long trek through the desert to the promised land, they built little huts, or tabernacles, called "succos" for shelter on the way, and these give their name to the day. It could equally well have been called the Festival of Manna, their heaven-sent daily bread on the journey.

In December, Hanukkah, the Festival of Lights, ushers in a season of rejoicing lasting for eight days. The lighted candles celebrate one of their few victories as a people. It was the victory gained for them by Judah Maccabee over the Syrians, a victory which made possible their return to Jerusalem. There, when they were cleansing the temple, preparatory to renewal of worship, they found a single unopened cask of oil, sufficient to burn before the altar for eight days. Each year as the candles burn for eight days in the Festival of Lights, the Jews reenact their past and are made one by it. But since, like Christmas, it has become also a time for friendly greetings and the exchange of gifts, it also strengthens bonds of friendship and reinforces family ties.

Purim, usually celebrated in March, is a gay and noisy day of triumph. By the retelling of the dramatic story of Queen Esther, the beautiful Jewish wife of a Persian King, who in a melodrama of court intrigue managed to turn Haman's plot against the Jews into his own downfall, every child in the synagogue shares in Queen Esther's courage and success as if it all happened yesterday. The children are permitted to use noisemakers to drown out every utterance of Haman's name, which helps to collapse the intervening years into nothingness and makes them co-actors with the Queen.

The Passover, which comes roughly at Easter and sometimes coincides with its date, celebrates the season of the year when Moses led the children of Israel out of their Egyptian captivity. Specifically, it commemorates the night when the Angel of Death spared the first-born in each household if the lintel of the door was sprinkled with the blood of a lamb, as directed by Jehovah. In the morning, the Israelites left so hastily they had no time to leaven their bread. To this day, Jewish homes that observe ritual eat unleavened bread, delicious "Matzos," and bitter herbs for a period of eight days to help them "remember" as individuals what they as a group learned so long ago.

Unique among religious festivals is the annual Jewish celebration of Shavuos, which commemorates God's gift of the Torah, the sacred book of laws, to Moses. The Torah is the central core of Jewish worship. It is a Holy of Holies. The reverence shown it is homage for a God who personifies the law and order of the universe. The yearly impressive celebration of Shavuos may perchance help to explain the preponderance of great thinkers, philosophers, and scientists among the Jews, who have enshrined the Torah, the symbol of law and order, in their Holy of Holies.

"As a man thinketh in his heart, so is he" is a profound truth, but it is no less profoundly true that every act a person performs helps to make him what he is. If the act becomes habitual it tends to mark the outline of personality. We fashion and shape a social environment, and it ends by shaping us. The rendezvous we have with destiny is shaped in no small measure by such seemingly insignificant things as gadgets, gestures, and the calendar.

CHAPTER XI

Monstrous Gods

There were religions whose gods were so essentially evil that they had no need for a devil as well. Their monstrous gods were objects of worship because they inspired fear. Fear of enemies and illness, and fear for the tomorrow which follows death with uncertainties even greater, inspired the offerings of appeasement on their altars.

There were also gods who were used by their followers to help them conquer neighboring peoples. It was a military asset for the fierce Aztecs that they had the god Huitzitopochtli on their side. Their enemies knew that if they were captured, the Aztecs would cut their hearts from their living bodies and fling them still quivering on the ever-hot stones of Huitzitopochtli's altar. Through the years prisoners of war and conquered neighbors kept the god well-nourished, and the god in turn kept the neighbors in abject fear.

Many students of comparative religion are convinced that fear is the root of religious practice and belief, and this theory is often coupled with the theory that religions have evolved from animalistic beliefs about natural objects and events. It is easy to see that awe-inspiring or threatening aspects of nature, not understood by primitive peoples, could cause them to try to appease alien powers felt to be hostile. And as we know Islam did not invent the practise of saying to a conquered people, "Accept our faith or die," we can readily understand the rapid spread of the faith of a strong, warlike group.

We know from Prescott's account of *The Conquest of Mexico* that the Aztecs were not primitive people when Cortes encountered them. Their priests were learned astronomers. Their architectural skills were noteworthy and their craftsmanship in metals and fabrics was amazing, and yet it has been estimated that over 136,000 victims were offered on Huitzitopochtli's altar. It is difficult to reckon how very many maidens were thrown into the sacred well of Chichén Itzá centuries before the Aztecs by the Mayans, and they, too, had a civilization at which we marvel.

The name of Molech has become a symbol of monster gods from the vivid accounts of his worship found in the Old Testament. There is a stern warning in Leviticus that any parent who gives his child to Molech shall himself be stoned to death. And yet his worship did not end. Babies were still thrown into his open mouth to fall into the blazing furnace of his belly. In First Kings there is a statement that King Solomon built an altar in a high place for Molech "the abomination of the children of Ammon" and "so did he for all his strange wives." From scattered references in other books of the Bible and from other sources, we know of the ghastly sacrifices to Molech. Priests selected firstborn sons about a year old, silken-haired and dimpled in all their appealing, trusting babyhood, and hurled them down in the gullet of the great image of the god to be consumed by fire in a blazing furnace. Why? Because the priests taught the people that they would themselves suffer intolerable ills unless the sacrifice was made. The people, in fear and terror and stupid belief, submitted.

No less a reference than the authoritative Encyclopedia Britannica in its latest edition, and it is no scandal sheet, records an interesting scientific surmise. It says that Molech or Maloch, it may be spelled either way, is a word made from the consonants of the Hebrew word for king and the vowels of the word for shame: hence probably a derogatory title for the god whom it was natural to think of as a ruler, a king. Furthermore, and this may well startle the reader, Molech was probably not a foreign god imported from the Ammonites, but Jahweh himself, degraded and contaminated by contact with other neighboring gods, until in the reigns of Ahaz and Manassah child sacrifices were offered to him. Indeed, more gods than we care to know may have demanded this most hideous tribute. We may forget that the Greek goddess Artemis, protectress of young things, in a dark and angry moment demanded the sacrifice of a fair young Greek girl upon her altar before she would permit the Greek fleet to set

Monstrous Gods 119

sail for Troy. The maiden was Iphigenia, a princess, the daughter of King Agamemnon.

It has long been customary, perhaps inevitable, for men to think of their deity, or deities, as rulers, monarchs, or kings with absolute power. Experience has tutored mankind in the belief that absolute power is ruthless, easily displeased, quick to anger, affronted by anything less than total subservience. It has been customary for victorious rulers to dispose of conquered peoples in two ways: they saved alive those useful to them in a condition of servitude, and they put to death those who might encumber them, including the very young. It was natural to expect a god to act in a royal, bloodthirsty fashion, he was the supreme embodiment of absolute power.

Even the Puritan poet Milton in his justly famous sonnet on his blindness endorses the idea of God's kingship. He wrote:

> his state
> Is kingly; thousands at his bidding speed
> And post o'er land and ocean without rest;
> They also serve who only stand and wait.

Fear of the gods and belief in monstrous gods who delight in blood and human sacrifice were not necessarily the outgrowth of animistic thinking on the part of primitive people but may rather have been a growing conviction of people tutored by the experience of political tyranny. The political climate men had created, not the death of summer's flowers, may have kept alive the world's monstrous gods.

We should not be astonished or dismayed to find evidence of the possible degeneration of a god such as the local war-god Yahweh into a god of evil, the equivalent of a devil, while at the same time we are aware that at the hands of law-givers like Moses, social reformers like the prophets, and poets like the psalmists he is evolving into the One God, clothed in majesty and ruling in righteousness. After all, deviltry and divinity have a common root; and language, no less than rock strata, yields significant fossils. It is well known for instance that the gods of conquered peoples, when not assimilated into the religion of the conquering nation, have frequently suffered transformation into devils as a convenient form of religious banishment.

It is not merely possible, but also probable, that fear of cataclysmic natural events such as earthquakes has blended with the concept of capricious tyrannical power to augment the worship of abhorrent gods. This would help to explain the inhumanity of the worship of Poseidon in ancient Crete. The most prized postcard which visitors to the Island of Crete mail to fortunate friends is a reproduction of a colorful mural from the recently excavated labyrinth in the Palace of Knossos on Crete. It depicts bull-dancers, boys and girls pitted against charging bulls with no defense against the bulls except their agility in leaping at the thrust of the sharp horns. The mural yields historical authenticity to an ancient legend which portrays a grim aspect of Greek religion. We usually think of Greek gods in full sunlight, often, it must be admitted with deplorable morals and unbecoming jealousies, but not as bloodthirsty monsters.

It is true that Saturn, a more primitive, older god, before the Olympians, had a habit of devouring his own children, but perhaps that was only an allegorical way of saying that the past lives in the present. However, Poseidon, the earth-shaker, was another matter. It was a matter of religious belief that only fair human flesh could appease him and prevent him from sending frequent devastating earthquakes to the Island of Crete with a great toll in human life. Bulls were sacred to Poseidon, and bulls, bred for strength and rage, with long cruelly pointed horns, were appropriate instruments for goring sacrificial victims to death. The sacrifice became an exciting spectacle for the spectators looking down upon the bull-pit. Both bulls and victims were resplendent in jewels and color. The sacrifice was made into a game, a dance of life or death, by training the boys and girls how to meet the bull. They were taught to stand their ground to the last second as the bull charged at them, to grasp a horn as he lowered his head, and by its help vault to safety, sometimes on his back, sometimes over him. Many escaped death, sometimes for a year or more,

Monstrous Gods

and became favorites of the cheering crowd who, like the gods, enjoyed courage and skill as well as bloodshed.

Yearly, however, Crete, a warlike island, had to exact tribute from weaker subjugated states and islands to replenish depleted reserves of victims. Even Athens sent its annual tribute of seven young men and seven unblemished maidens for the Palace of Knossos. Those who became most skilled and most agile were sent into the pit time after time, armed only with their courage, to face the bull of death. There was always that last fatal time when the sharp horns impaled them, one after another, and Poseidon was satisfied.

When, a few paragraphs back, I hesitated to affix the label "monstrous" to Greek gods, I was over-generous. The tortures which Zeus ordained for Prometheus were nothing short of monstrous. Prometheus' crime was that he acted as benefactor to mankind. According to Greek and Roman legends of creation, men were the last living beings to be created and were put together of the scraps of what was left over after such magnificent animals as lions, eagles, and great scale-covered reptiles had been fully equipped. Man was naked, puny of strength, without claws or great teeth, feathers or fur, very vulnerable and entirely miserable.

Prometheus, a Titan and one of the older gods, saw and pitied the wretched estate of man and sought to remedy his lot. He was the first great humanitarian. He stole fire from the great flaming altar of the sun itself, and with the gift of fire gave man the first comfort he had ever known. More than that, he gave man the means of bettering his condition. With fire as his tool, man could remake his difficult dwelling place into a near-Paradise to rival Olympus.

Apparently Zeus felt it was imperative for the prestige of the gods that the difference between those who had and those who had not should remain. He seized the benefactor of man, branded him a rebel to god, chained him to the highest, most bleak crag in the Caucasus, and sent a vulture to tear at his liver. As Prometheus was immortal, the liver continually renewed itself.

Prometheus, chained to the wind-swept mountain peak, in utter solitude endured the unending agony of dying without the grace of death, and because he had aroused the implacable anger of Zeus, became himself a symbol of self-sacrifice, a savior-god, while Zeus became a symbol of tyranny.

Many of the other Olympian gods and goddesses had dual natures, even as they had more than one name. Thus Artemis, a pure maiden goddess, protectress of the helpless, the young, and wildlife, goddess of the light of the moon, was known also as Hecate, goddess of the dark of the moon, patroness of evil, goddess of the danger which lurks at the crossway.

A Roman poet named Titus Lucretius Carus, known to us as Lucretius, born probably in 96 B.C., tried to save his fellow Romans from the fear of terrible gods. He died tragically by his own hand on October 15, 55 B.C., when he was only forty-one. Tradition says that he had become crazed by a love-philter administered by his jealous and superstitious wife. During his brief life he became a profound and devoted student of the teachings of the Greek philosopher Epicurus. He was convinced that only when men became acquainted with the truth of Epicurus' thorough-going materialism could they rid themselves of fear. He glimpsed the massive security implicit in the indifferent universe of natural law, where no god's whims could raise a storm or calm a sea. He pitied men for their fear of the anger of the gods and despised them for grovelling to curry favor. For him the Latin word *religio* was synonymous with superstition. Moreover, he followed Epicurus in his teaching that men torment themselves needlessly with fears of endless suffering after death. Only the atoms which compose both soul and body are immortal, Lucretius wrote, and after death, the atoms of the soul as well as those of the body are dispersed in the void. Death has no more significance than the quenching of a flame: it was, and then it is not.

In the great poem, six books or chapters in length, which Lucretius called *De Rerum Natura* or *Concering the Nature of Things*, he reasoned usually by analogy—and often with what seem to the modern reader fantastic results. However, he was attempting an empirical approach, and everyday experience was

Monstrous Gods 123

the only laboratory open for his observations. His explanation of the cause of earthquakes is an example in point. Incidentally, they were common enough in Italy to keep alive the superstitious belief that they were caused because some person or some city had incurred the wrath of earth-shaking Poseidon, and their recurrence could be prevented only by sacrifice. Lucretius, following Epicurus, says that the earth below us is similar to its surface. It has caves, and lakes, and streams. An earthquake is caused by the collapse beneath the surface of some great cavern wall, or results when some great boulder in mid-earth rolls into a subterranean lake. Also, a mighty wind, he thought, might become "entangled" in a cavern, and escaping, burst through the surface forming a crack or chasm, attended by a trembling. This is more than a fantastic guess, it is a working hypothesis needing testing, refinement, correction, and ultimately rewording in terms of stress and tension, after scientists acquired knowledge of earth's strata to replace the fancied duplication of the landscape of the surface.

Lucretius endeavored to minimize volcanic eruptions (which insurance companies still classify as "Acts of God") by two means. He says men think them supernatural because they seem so vast and cause such tremendous devastation. This seeming vastness, Lucretius said, is a relative matter: Consider how much more vast "the sum of things" is, and how infinitely small a portion of the universe our "one heaven" is. The "void," he said, is infinite. An eruption on Mt. Etna, he wrote, is like some "passing" illness to the human frame. It may be caused by "wind entangled with heat" within the hollow depth of the crater.

One is tempted to compare Lucretius' courage in writing thus with the courage of the great Chieftainess Kapiolani of the Sandwich Islands, now Hawaii, in freeing her people from the fear of Peelé. The priests of the terrible goddess Peelé who dwelt, they said, in the boiling lava in the volcanic crater of Kilauea on Maui, predicted that if Kapiolani should climb, as she proposed to do, to the crater's rim and hurl into it the scarlet berries sacred to Peelé, the goddess in her wrath would destroy the island. Kapiolani, recently a convert to Christianity, climbed to the rim in spite of them, hurled the scarlet berries in defiance, and thus freed her people from their age-long fear of hideous Peelé.

But to return to Lucretius, in writing his didactic poem, Lucretius acknowledged his debt to Epicurus, "a master whom he held divine," and Epicurus in turn was indebted to Democritus, "The Laughing Philosopher" of the third century B.C. Thus Lucretius' materialistic explanation of the origin and nature of the universe is very old and is the logical alternative to a supernatural explanation. Lucretius began with the limitless void of space and, moving through it, an unlimited number of invisible particles of matter called atoms. They were, however, of a limited number of shapes and sizes. Their everlasting sameness and indivisibility was their guarantee of immortality. This divine dust was uncreated and indestructible, and the atoms which constituted it were the ultimate building blocks of all that is: of man and of his mind, of mountains and of streams, of the wind, the sun, yes even of the gods, if indeed there were gods in a remote region of their own, beyond any possible contact with or influence on man.

The infinite and ever-changing variety of objects given us in sensory experience was due, he wrote, to the ability of atoms to form different clusters, larger or smaller aggregates, as the hooks with which they were equipped intermeshed as they moved and collided or recoiled in the void. As our modern poet A. E. Housman wrote in perfect accord with Lucretius' thought:

> The stuff of life to knit me
> Blew hither: here am I.

It was incumbent on Lucretius to discuss the nature and the power of the gods, as the purpose of his didactic poem was to free man not only from the fear of death and the fabled terrors awaiting him beyond the River Acheron, but also from the fear of the gods while living. Lucretius believed that only when freed from the needless anxieties thrust upon him by baseless religious beliefs could man attain that serenity of mind that enables him to enjoy the simple, natural pleasures attendant upon health such as sound sleep following vigorous activity, the enjoyment of the beauty of morning and evening, cold water from a hillside spring, and time to think. Such were the pleasures Epicurus had proclaimed in his secluded garden as the proper goals of life, and such Lucretius hoped to secure again for the jaded, harried Romans of the hectic reign of Sulla, who feared the displeasure of the gods while living and their punishment after death.

Lucretius was certain that the sure knowledge that nothing exists except atoms, the void, and motion was indeed a truth to make men free of fear. If there are gods he said, a possibility he considered because of the widespread belief in them, they, too, can be nothing but clusters of atoms, and so like all "clusters" or "things" subject to dissolution.

Tennyson's poem called "Lucretius" is a faithful poetic statement following closely Lucretius' own statement of their nature and their abode. Tennyson wrote:

> The gods who haunt
> The lucid interspace of world and world,
> Where never creeps a cloud or moves a wind,
> Nor ever falls the least white star of snow
> Nor ever roll of thunder moans
> Nor sound of human sorrow mounts to mar
> Their sacred ever-lasting calm.

These indifferent gods "lying beside their nectar, careless of mankind" did not need to be reckoned with. Man could be as indifferent to them as they were to him. They were very different, too, from a god who still has altars in our modern world, a god who is considered capable of "visiting the iniquities of the fathers upon the children upon the third and upon the fourth generation." When, in the middle of the eighteenth century, Jonathan Edwards, an eloquent divine, filled a Congregational pulpit in Northampton, Massachusetts, members of his congregation began an hysterical exodus from his parish to save their lives. Each was afraid he or she might be the next to commit suicide if he or she remained in Northampton. Such famous sermons as the one called "Sinners in the hands of an angry God" filled those who heard him preach with such terror of God's righteous anger and such conviction of their finite worthlessness before the blaze of infinite perfection that, like moths, one after another sought refuge in the flame of swift extinction. Whatever else Jonathan Edwards, later president of Princeton College, demonstrated, he made clear the intolerable cruelty of a standard of absolute perfection. When religious leaders think like Jonathan Edwards that they can serve God and man by proclaiming God's infinite and absolute perfection, they create an ideal before which "good" in human, measurable terms shrivels into nothingness and leaves us naked before a god who is monstrous because morally devastating.

For the Platonists of our day who see nothing monstrous in absolute perfection, let me hasten to add there are still gods about who are "monstrous" in the limited positive fashion in which the term is commonly understood. *Island Possessed,* a book written by the cultured anthropologist and dancer Katherine Dunham and published in 1969 by Doubleday, contains a remarkable account of the author's initiation into voodoo, or as she prefers to name it *vaudun.*

Her initiation put her under the protection of the serpent-god Damballa, with whom she was regarded as having contracted a spiritual marriage. The religious concept of spiritual marriage to a god is not uniquely part of Haitian voodoo, as the parallel concept of "bride of Heaven" or "bride of Christ" plays a vital role in much Christian thinking.

Because she is an American mulatto, and in spite of the fact that she is a college-trained woman doing serious research, after prolonged residence in Haiti Katherine Dunham found herself gradually and subtly drawn into a position where she was eligible for initiation into the first of the three mystic levels of voodoo.

According to her own graphic account, the initiation was a gruesome ordeal lasting three days and nights. She was one of a group of nine candidates of both sexes and varying ages initiated into the cult of Rada-Dahome. The ceremony was a "head-cleansing" or *lavé tete.* She was told in advance by the priestess in charge that the god who would possess her was no other than

Monstrous Gods

Damballa, the mighty serpent god. Like many gods, including Jehovah, he is considered a jealous god, and while he protects his chosen devotees and grants them many powers including clairvoyance, he is quick to anger and avenges unfaithfulness in dire ways.

In spite of the fact that Miss Dunham failed to develop the ecstasy leading to convulsions and the ability to speak with tongues, she danced her way into the abandon of the final mysteries of the ritual in which the god possessed his chosen.

And this took place not at a spot remote from the shores of America, but in the Caribbean, not centuries ago, but twenty-some years ago, and is not a matter of hearsay but the authenticated account of an educated person, trained to observe and report. The account is filed in the archives of her university.

CHAPTER XII

Pious Cloaks

Many times in the history of the world vehement religious fanaticism has been a cloak for greed and an excuse for cruelty. The hypocrites who in the name of religion have exploited, murdered, raped, enslaved, plundered and tortured other human beings, although deserving to stand on the lowest rung of the ladder of infamy, have often been admired. They have been hailed as leaders and as champions and heroes. Thousands have followed them. Other thousands have died for them.

Take for example Mohmud of the Kingdom of Ghanzi in Afghanistan, in the years between 1001 and 1027 A.D. He was a chieftain descended from a long line of Turkish rulers, who made seventeen raids upon the rich Indian plains adjacent to his kingdom. He made these raids on the pretext of spreading the Islamic faith and converting Hindus from the worship of false gods. After each raid, long caravans of booty and chained gangs of slaves made their way back to his capital at Ghanzi. He looted Indian palaces, desecrated and robbed Hindu temples, and plundered public buildings "to the glory of Allah" and his own profit. His raids are well-authenticated examples of holy wars rather than isolated historical events.

Later, in the sixteenth and seventeenth centuries, the use the Turks made of enslaved Christians to fight holy wars against other Christians, some of them their kin, was ingenious and devilish, and highly successful. It was against sacred law to enslave fellow Moslems, and yet the Sultan as "Defender of the Faith" and "Shadow of God on Earth" needed trustworthy armies of Moslem zealots to hold the vast Ottoman Empire together with its outposts in Europe, Asia, and Africa dangerously far-flung.

The Turks solved the problem by carefully educating and training young Christian slaves to do the job for them. These

Pious Cloaks

were the famous Jannissaries, Christian boys taken from their homes while still children and enslaved. Some twelve thousand of them formed a special fighting order. They were forbidden to marry. They were trained exclusively as warriors, and indoctrination raised their zeal for Allah to fever pitch. They inspired more fear than ever Caesar's Tenth Legion did, for they regarded their adversaries as devils fighting Allah—not as simple barbarians defending their homes. They were as innocent of pity as was the steel of their curved scimitars.

In Frazer's *Golden Bough* there is a sinister account of pious fraud by means of which murder was made to appear the service of God. Frazer, in his account, was quoting from a book published in 1880 by Zwifel and Monstier and called *Voyage Aux Sources du Niger*. Frazer says that the leaders of the savage Timmes tribe of Sierra Leone had perfected a scheme for ridding themselves of any man against whom they, the leaders, had a dislike or grudge. They chose him king, but on the pretext of purifying their king of all sin, they reserved to themselves the right to administer a ceremonial religious beating to the king on the eve of his coronation. It was a matter of record that a surprising number of kings died immediately following their coronations.

The Crusades were, of course, the best known examples of holy wars. They spanned an incredible number of centuries after the First Crusade began in 1095, and they dwindled into disrepute in the middle of the fifteen century. The First Crusade was sanctioned by Pope Urban II, and successive crusades were sanctioned by a succession of Popes, until their dwindling success in 1254, when Louis IX of France returned more ravaged than triumphant, led people to suspect God was not fighting on their side. The avowed purpose of the First Crusade was to wrest the Holy Sepulcher from the Turks, and it was undertaken with religious fervor at white heat with throngs of pilgrims escorting the armies led by knights who as counts and dukes commanded the feudal forces under their control.

In the preface to the English edition of Zoe Oldenbourg's scholarly book *The Crusades*, published in 1966, she speaks of the glory of that first Crusade. In her opinion what she refers to as the "mirage" of the Holy City Jerusalem and its rescue, which was to involve more or less deeply the conscience of all of Catholic Christendom, was a glory which defies time in spite of the prolonged sufferings and the atrocities that accompanied it. That is one point of view.

It is true that one of the immediate causes of the First Crusade was the interruption of pilgrim traffic to holy places and in particular to the Holy Sepulcher in Jerusalem. After the victory of the Seljuk Turks in the battle of Manzikert in 1071, nomadic bands of Turks began to raid pilgrim bands crossing Anatolia on their way to Jerusalem. As pilgrimage to holy places was accepted in Christianity, as it has been in many other religions, as one of the most direct routes to heavenly bliss, its interruption was felt as a grievous thing. This harassment, felt by the laity in particular, coincided with a vigorous stirring within the ranks of the clergy called the Cluniac movement. This movement, which was strongest in Benedictine monasteries, called for greater devotion to the faith as well as stern and pure self-discipline. Pilgrimages were recommended as one form of self-discipline. Possibly the greatest influence favoring the First Crusade was the leadership of Pope Urban II.

It was his dearest wish to heal the schism that had, since 1054, divided the Latin Catholic Church centered in Rome from the Greek Orthodox Church with St. Sophia in Constantinople its administrative center. Both accepted the creed as formulated by the Council of Nicea. They were divided on hierarchical and administrative lines rather than by creed. After 1054, as rival churches they had had to cope with different enemies from without. The Latin Church managed to assimilate their Norman foes. The Greek Orthodox Church was less successful against the Turks of Mongol origin who were predominantly adherents of Islam. They held political domination over what had been the Byzantine Empire.

So it was that when, in 1095, the Byzantine Emperor Alexius Commenus wrote to Pope Urban II asking aid against the Turks, the Pope welcomed the invitation as a means for healing the **break between the two churches, with protection of pilgrimage and the rescue of the Holy Sepulcher as secondary reasons.**

Pious Cloaks

Although the reasons leading Pope Urban II to bless the First Crusade were largely political, the reasons that recruited vast throngs of fighters to follow the banners of the leaders of the Crusade were religious. For them it was a holy war, fought to restore sacred places to Christian control and to permit freedom of pilgrimage to these holy places when once they had been restored to reverent hands.

The Crusade began with waving standards and the awe-inspiring marching of thousands of determined men led by armored knights riding their proud steeds. In the weeks and months and years ahead it endured weary, dusty marches, bivouacked on windy uplands, took food from a ravished countryside, plundered, fought and, by the hundreds, died.

The important medieval city of Antioch, a center of culture and wealth, withstood a long and bloody siege. Only after its fall did the Crusaders finally capture Jerusalem on a hot July day. At last the Holy Sepulcher was in Christian hands—in Christian hands which did not flinch from their religious duty to massacre without mercy the Moslems and Jews, enemies of true religion, who had so long stood in their path. Christians kept the sepulcher for ten years.

The First Crusade had set the pattern for the Second. It was undertaken in answer to a plea by Pope Eugenius III to complete unfinished conquest. Louis VII of France took the standard of the cross to lead his armies and was joined by a German king, Conrad III, who had been inflamed with holy zeal by the impassioned preaching of Bernard of Clairvaux, one of the greatest evangelists of all time. Of this crusade, as of the first, it has been written in many chronicles that it was marked by "corruption, greed and disaster."

Meanwhile, the Moslems, though temporarily beaten, were far from crushed. They, in turn, instituted holy wars of their own called jihads. Imad-al-Din, or Zinge, attacked and recaptured Damascus and later Edessa. Both places, after their capture by crusaders, had been established as feudal strongholds ruled by Christian counts, to the rulers' own economic advantage. On October 2, 1187, Saladin, the great Moslem leader, preceded his victorious army into Jerusalem.

Popes Gregory VIII and Clement III called for a new crusade to reverse the rising tide of Islamic victory, and accordingly the Third Crusade was launched with leaders from England, France, and Germany. There was Richard I, the "lion-hearted," from England; Philip II (Augustus) of France; and Frederick I, known as Barbarossa (the red beard) who was not only a German king but also emperor of the Holy Roman Empire. From the first they disagreed; and in the final outcome only Richard could boast of victories, and they were hard-won.

In the Sixth Crusade, Emperor Frederick II, whose title was also King of Sicily, was severely reprimanded by the papacy because in February 1229 he acquired Jerusalem, Bethlehem, Nazareth, and Sidon, together with intervening territory and a ten-year peace from the Sultan of Egypt by careful diplomacy instead of good honest fighting such as is incumbent on a soldier of the cross.

The Seventh Crusade was somewhat like a small private sally. Louis IX of France "took the cross" in December 1244 because of ardent personal convictions regarding the obligation of chivalrous Christianity and to fulfill a vow made when he had feared he was dying. It was a dismal crusade. Indeed, the final crusades were all of diminishing vigor because of diminishing conviction unless we include as a crusade, as historians do not, Christopher Columbus' voyage of discovery, which he assured his royal sponsors would "help to circumvent the Moslems of the Eastern Mediterranean," among other aims.

One of the seldom recognized consequences of the Crusades was the intensification of anti-Semitism. In much the same way as animated cartoons on the screen create stereotypes for viewers today, so the miracle and morality plays of the Middle Ages created stereotypes of possibly even greater impact. The plays had the sanction and blessing of the church and thus for the mass of viewers carried the imprint "gospel true." In these plays a Jew seldom had an individual name but appeared in the cast of characters simply as "a Jew." In every way he was made to look as much like the current representation of Satan as possible, for of course the Jews had to be villains, as Jews had crucified Jesus. The Crusaders had increased mass belief in Jewish guilt for the crucifixion, and as a consequence the identification of the Jews with Satan grew firmer in proportion as the devotion to Jesus and places identified with his passion increased.

The malicious stereotype of Jewish traits fostered by these plays was carried by Crusaders into remote parts of Europe and Asia. Echoes of the superstitions thus engendered and spread reverberate around the world even today. In the August 13, 1967, issue of the Asian Magazine, an article on Macao, the once thriving Portuguese city on an island adjacent to Hong Kong, reports such an echo. In its proud days as a thriving Portuguese port, well-trained Jesuit priests presided over most of the island's schools. In 1762 the Chinese expelled most of the Jesuits; only a few Jesuit teachers remained. The article said they were for the most part illiterate and superstitious priests who indoctrinated their Portuguese pupils with the superstition rampant in the Middle Ages that Jewish babies were born with tails as punishment for the Jewish rôle in the crucifixion of Christ. Their kinship to Satan was evident, so the children of Macao were taught as late as 1967.

One of the strangest and most virulent beliefs which poisoned the Middle Ages and was undoubtedly a factor in making possible Hitler's attempt to exterminate the Jews as a people was the legend of Anti-Christ. In a learned and carefully documented book called *The Devil and the Jews,* copyrighted in 1943 by the Yale University Press, Joshua Trachtenberg has a most informative chapter on the subject of Anti-Christ. It is worth reading by anyone wishing to realize the extremes the imagination can reach when inspired by fear and nourished by false piety.

Anti-Christ, who, if not Satan himself, was supposed to be Satan-begotten, was identified with the Messiah for whose coming the Jews still hoped. He was also "The Adversary" of legend, who with an army of demons would be on hand to oppose Christ and his angels at the second coming, said confidently to be near at hand. It was a tenacious and widespread belief. Such notable scholastics as Thomas Aquinas and Albertus Magnus discussed it gravely and with credulity. The Latin Anti-Christ plays of the thirteenth century made it vividly impressive for large and receptive audiences. Trachtenberg noted that as late as 1469 the

Frankfort City Council established special protection for the Jewish Quarter of the city whenever such a play was given. Rumors of the actual birth of Anti-Christ, circumstantial, frequent, and lewd, kept Christendom in terror from the end of the thirteenth century onward.

In the sixteenth century, the legendary Ahasuerus, better known as the "Wandering Jew," was reported to have made a sudden visit to the principal cities of Europe and increased the terror, for it was well known that his long ordeal of flight would end in the mercy of death only at the Second Coming. Everyone knew the legend must be true.

Trachtenberg's book elucidates other matters which, under the guise of piety, led to the persecution of the Jews. Such a phrase as "the odor of sanctity" seems to most of us mere metaphorical speech. Not so. For the Middle Ages it was a literal description of the fragrance emanating from a baptized person, living or dead, in contrast to the stench of a "demonic" Jew. Sometimes that stench was said to be a mixture of brimstone and sulphur, if the Jew's Satanic connections were to be emphasized, for many people believed the Jews to be actually the devil incarnate. At other times the odor was more like the odor of a billy-goat, the devil's favorite mount and the animal which in cathedral sculpture Jews are most frequently portrayed as riding, facing backward.

Even the wisdom of Solomon became a reproach to the Jews as a people. It branded them as alchemists, astrologers, magicians, and sorcerers. General credence was given to a Jew's possession of a magic ring, "King Solomon's ring," which enabled the wearer to understand the speech of animals. Jews in general, even without rings, were known in the Middle Ages to possess occult knowledge and to use it to their own advantage. Jews who studied medicine were suspected of being in the profession in order to poison Christians, and no less illustrious a person than Queen Elizabeth I had her physician, a converted Jew, Rodrigo Lopez, executed on the charge of having tried to poison her. Even then, the world was preparing for Puritan Salem, Massachusetts, with its witchcraft and its own unholy "holy war."

It is with difficulty that the Inquisition, or more properly the

Pious Cloaks

Inquisitions, can be differentiated from the Crusades or the persecution of the Jews in medieval times. All were the products of bigotry. It is exceedingly difficult when one is preoccupied with the hideous sufferings of both the Crusaders and their victims, with the spiritual humiliations and bodily injuries inflicted on the Jews, and with the torture chambers and burnings at the stake of heretics, to remember that the bigots responsible felt they were doing God's will, or at best some of them did. Others must have known their motives were mixed and must have hoped fervently that neither their world nor posterity would suspect the truth.

One of the instruments devised in the Middle Ages to insure the steadfastness and unswerving purity of religious beliefs was the Holy Office, popularly known as the Inquisition. At first penalties for heresy were spiritual only, generally excommunication, but after Theodosius I (the Great) made Christianity the established religion, late in the fourth century, heretics became also enemies of the state. Thereupon laws were enacted to establish penalties for such civil disobedience that included confiscation of property, a valuable weapon against wealthy Jews who refused baptism, and later exile and loss of civil rights, ultimately the loss of life.

It was extraordinarily easy even for a person who in all sincerity thought he was a good Christian to be a heretic, for the creed which bishops had adopted at Nicea in 325 when Constantine summoned them to settle the dispute about the nature of Christ was very exact and explicit. Arius had debated with Athanasius the question: Was Christ of the same or of similar nature to God? After Nicea if you said "similar," you were a heretic. Or if you said of the Son of God that before he was begotten he was not, you were a heretic. If you regarded God as a single being and the three persons as aspects of God, you were a Sabellian heretic. Anyone who thought God the Father entered into Jesus and suffered the pangs of death on the cross with him was another variety of heretic, a Patri-passion. One gross type of heresy was Apollinarian, to believe Jesus was all Logos and not really human. And if, taking a cautious attitude on the difficult problem, you held that Mary can have been mother only to that which was human in Jesus, you became a Nestorian heretic. In the process of clearly labeling and anathematizing the heresies, the doctrine of the Trinity was firmly entrenched.

For many of us the word Inquisition is synonymous with torture chambers and burnings at the stake, but it was not until 1022 that Robert II of France had 13 heretics burned at the stake at Orleans. Thereafter the brutality of the medieval Inquisition increased, largely because of an order to the effect that rulers who failed to act vigorously to rid their realms of heretics would be deposed. Thereupon, the rulers, one after another, decreed the death penalty for heresy: Aragon in 1190, Rome in 1230, Germany in 1232, and others at intervals between. Pope Gregory IX, fearing the Inquisition might become entirely a political instrument, with a religious disguise, restricted trials for heresy to the church. Dominican monks usually did the investigating. Torture during interrogation was forbidden until 1252, when Innocent IV issued a papal bull permitting it.

At first, too, sentences for heresy were relatively mild. Convicted heretics were sentenced to say prayers, to fast, to go on pilgrimages or obliged to give alms. Then they increased in severity. Heretics were flogged. They were imprisoned, sometimes for life, without knowing their accuser. Sometimes they suffered all these punishments plus the confiscation of their property. When, however, the death penalty was imposed on hardened cases, who stubbornly refused to recant or to be baptised, it was imposed by civil, not church, authority. The church kept its hands clean. Among the hardened cases we come upon these names: Joan of Arc, John Huss, and Girolamo Savonarola.

In the late fourteenth century, the Inquisition in Spain became particularly cruel and took on a racial aspect. More than two thousand Jews who refused to become "Marranos," i.e., converts to the faith, were burned at the stake. Others fled. After the Jews, the Moslems who had settled in Spain and then the Protestants fell in the purge. Doubtless the instigators of the horrors felt justified, for they argued that to corrupt the faith and rob men of heaven is a more serious crime than to counterfeit money and rob them of mere worldly wealth.

A gentle and noble heretic who fell victim to the Roman Inquisition and was burned at the stake in 1600 was Giordano Bruno, the last victim to die this fiery death. At fifteen he had entered the Dominican order, but thirteen years later discarded his Dominican garb because he had been indiscreet enough to defend the Aryan heresy. He fled to Rome, then to Geneva, and finally to England, where he found welcome in the circle of wits around Sir Philip Sidney. As a true child of the Renaissance he trusted reason and was not frightened by magnitude. He became a pantheist with a conception of God very like the Hindu conception of Brahma. He believed the world was infinite, that there were indeed an infinite number of worlds beside our Earth, and that they came from a cause of infinite power and goodness.

He understood God as a universal power, or providence, whereby each thing moves and grows according to its nature. He explained this in two ways, one as the way the soul is in the body and the other as the ineffable way in which God is omnipresent in a fashion beyond our understanding. This he was asked to recant. Recant this, he would not do. Just so Jesus, in whose name so many were burned at the stake, was martyred by the collusion of two great forces: orthodoxy and the political order. For Jesus, the young and incorruptible social rebel, so troublesome to the established order, was crucified on the charge of blasphemy.

Motives are notoriously hard to fathom. We are sometimes shocked into the realization that our own motives are mixed, sometimes to the extent that an unworthy motive, which we had not acknowledged even to ourselves, has been cloaked by a praiseworthy one. Thus, like the inscriptions on memorial windows that should sometimes read "to the glory of the donor and in memory of God," our motives are seldom clearly stated. There is ample historical evidence, as in instances cited in this chapter, that rulers or groups in power have often manipulated masses of people by appealing to religious motives to accomplish ends motivated by considerations quite other than religious. It is so easy and usually much safer to be a hypocrite than to acknowledge greedy and revengeful purposes; besides, men fancy that a pious cloak becomes them.

CHAPTER XIII

Women, Adored and Abhorred

Epochs, as well as men, have registered ambivalent feelings about woman. She has been, and is, both adored and abhorred, worshipped and scorned. She has been worshipped as the goddess she isn't and maligned as the root of all evil. Her status in society fluctuates with the various attitudes she elicits. They, in turn, influence the structure of the family, largely determine the laws of marriage and the forms of courtship, and deeply influence religious concepts.

Both St. Matthew and St. Mark are explicit in declaring, on the authority of Jesus, that in the life after death, men and women "neither marry nor are given in marriage but are as angels in heaven." Angels are sexless, in spite of their masculine names, which are of course necessary to indicate superior beings.

The Koran, just as explicitly, states that on the last day, when the great trumpet has sounded, when the heavens have split asunder and the mountains have been ground to dust, the graves will open and men and women, attended by their guardian angels, will be called to account. Each resurrected person's deeds, recorded in the book of his life, will be weighed in the balance. If he is damned, the book will then be placed in his left hand; if blessed, in his right. Then the blessed, both men and women, will be summoned to enter the Garden of Paradise, the Abode of Peace, which is a green oasis sustained by ever-flowing rivers. Lying on silk-draped couches, the blessed will forever enjoy heavenly food and drink and sexual dalliance. Wives of perfect purity and the houri, dark-eyed maidens, miraculously and eternally virgins, will make life an unending paradise for men.

It is not unusual for attitudes toward sexual behavior to differ not only between religions but within a religion. There are

Women, Adored and Abhorred

records of religious attitudes, poles apart, which have hardened into religious law. Thus, in the past some religions have made it mandatory that every woman at least once in her life should offer herself in the service of a god as a temple prostitute, and religions have also sanctioned, by religious law, stoning to death any woman found in adultery.

It is possible to ascertain, with a high degree of certainty, the sexual convictions of the adherents of a religion by subjecting its religious literature, including its myths and legends, to an analysis known to psychologists as a projective technique. When free to create his gods, how has man imagined the objects of his worship? It is instructive to begin with Zeus, who was a lusty god, more noted for his amorous exploits than for his wisdom, although even in Zeus there exists an ambivalence. His favorite child was Pallas Athena, literally his brain child, for she sprang motherless from his forehead and not from his loins. To her, he entrusted his awful aegis and his buckler. She even carried his weapon of destruction, the thunderbolt. She, the gray-eyed maiden goddess, protected civilization as it expressed itself in the city and in the home. In the home, it was not the cradle over which she watched, it was the loom and the pottery wheel. Outside the home it was the culture of the fields over which she presided; plowing and seed time and harvest, not the increase of the herds and flocks. The olive which she created was her tree, the owl her bird, and the serene temple, the Parthenon, atop the Acropolis in Athens, was her shrine, a symbol of the proportioned beauty of wisdom.

Another maiden goddess was Artemis, the huntress, also daughter of Zeus and twin sister to Apollo. She was called also Silene, or in Latin, Luna, the chaste "protectress of dewey youth." She had another nature also, when as Silene, the moon goddess floating in silvery light over an upland pasture, she saw the beautiful shepherd Endymion, loved him at sight, and sought to seduce him with a kiss. But the kiss plunged Endymion into a sleep on his mountain glade on Latmus, though nightly he was wooed by the kisses of Silene. Artemis the huntress on earth is also Silene, moon goddess in the sky, and Hecate, dread goddess of evil doings in the dark of the moon. She is known also as the Goddess of the Crossways, protectress and even instigator of rape and of murder.

Ambivalence in regard to woman comes to the fore in Hindu religion in the two aspects, one benevolent, one grim, which are ascribed to the wife of Siva. In her kindly and virtuous aspect she is called most frequently by the name Parvate (Daughter of the Mountain). She is also called Mahadevi, which means simply "Great Goddess," or Sate, the virtuous one, or Gauri, the fair one. She may also be addressed as Annapurna, the bestower of ample food, or as the mother goddess, Mata Tamil Ammai.

In her horrible aspect, in which she is painted or carved as a repulsive hag, her name may be Durga, the inaccessible, or Kali, the black one, a demoness indeed. Or, she may be called Candi, the fierce one, with a huge lolling tongue, tusks for teeth, and skulls for ornaments.

These are all one and the same deity, the wife of Siva, who in his turn is one of the three gods of the Trimurti, a manifestation of Brahma. One encounters her different images throughout India in Hindu temples and shrines, solid and enduring evidence to the two diverse yet unresolved attitudes toward woman.

These carvings and the legends they exemplify make evident the ambivalence toward woman in Hindu religious art, in spite of the oft-remarked natural and frank acceptance of love between the sexes epitomized in the tenth-century statue of "The Lovers" from Khajaraho. Although it is executed in stone, no observer can fail to note the rapture of that close embrace of naked bodies. He will perhaps contrast it in his mind with an equally well-known Christian portrayal of the expulsion of Adam and Eve from the Garden. Adam and Eve, naked, too, except for fig leaves, walk side-by-side but icily apart, with bent heads, as if ashamed of their awareness they are male and female.

Feelings of sexual ambivalence have been wrought even more deeply into the structure of other religions. It is, for instance, central to the bewilderingly contradictory accounts of the paternity of Jesus. Was he, indeed, of royal David's line, or is Joseph who looks down pridefully in so many paintings of "the holy family" merely his foster-father? The assumption underlying the theory of the Immaculate Conception is that it would detract from Mary's purity and hence from her son's perfection if he had been normally conceived.

The feat of crowning Mary with both of the supreme titles of feminine adoration, "Mother" and "Virgin," could happen only because woman viewed as mother releases in people now mature the almost forgotten feelings of attachment and protection-seeking that were their bliss in childhood, while woman viewed as virgin elicits the rapturous elation of first possession, the pristine loveliness of buds just opening. A single word can carry a heavy freight of meaning. Such a word is "deflowered." The freight it carries are meanings abhorred—the ravaged, the desecrated, the spoiled. This assumed generalization, often unconscious, is implied in the Cult of the Virgin, even where the deflowered one is a wife.

The same ambivalence appears even more strikingly in the religious use of the word "Father." Christians are using the term of purest, trusting affection when they address God as "Our Father." That title of reverent adoration descends upon the Pope, as when he is regarded as God's representative on earth, he becomes "The Holy Father." Yet, this holy father may not marry. If he becomes a real father, he sullies the purity of his holiness. The conclusion can only be that marriage is not really a sacrament in spite of the prayer book. To be "of one flesh" is after all a rather vulgar thing. How can the Pope defend the mandatory celibacy of his priesthood as "the brilliant jewel" of the church, without at the same time erasing the word "holy" before matrimony?

Ambiguous use of labels in religion, as in the market place, can cause havoc in human relations. In some marriage services, there occur these words in the marriage vows: "with my body I thee worship," but the adjective "bodily" in its Latin form "carnal" has an ugly sound, and even when linked with a neutral word like "desire," it echoes in our ears with the loathsome word "lust."

Just as there are students of religion who find its source in fear and man's attempt to deal with that fear, there are others equally convinced the source of religion is the attempt to deal with problems arising out of the sexual instinct and its prohibitions. Many, like Freud, regard religion as the supreme sublimation of the sexual drive when civilization imposes restraints. Sublimation is, of course, the elevation of something base. The lotus blossom, as sublimated mud, is its perfect illustration—and particularly in Buddhist culture is so employed. And inevitably at the very center of the idea of sublimation there stands the contrast between the good and the bad, the high and the low, the permitted and the rejected. Imperfect sublimation may explain ambivalence.

There is another sense in which the sexual basis of religion is explained. Religion permits vicarious satisfaction. We all experience vicarious satisfaction when someone very near and very dear to us achieves his goal. Thus a parent can rejoice as if it were his own good fortune when his child's fondest hopes are realized. And thus, though a Greek citizen would have been punished by law for amorous exploits like those of Zeus or Apollo, he could enjoy them vicariously when he contemplated them in his gods, who were above the laws. Or the worshipper may go a bold step further, particularly if he feels himself rejected and misunderstood by his fellow men, a starveling for love. In mystic union he may feel himself the object of God's love, caught up in a moment of ecstatic union with the divine. It is a moment which is utterly private and which can be described only as "ineffable." A nun wears the wedding band of marriage to Christ.

It is significant to students of religion, who have been taught by Freud to use the term sexual in a wide sense, including the attachment of the libido to other members of the family and not exclusively to husband or wife, that this concept is useful in explaining the evaluation of religious concepts. Freud taught that an infant's emotional attachment, his libido, was first for his mother, then later for the father, progressing in maturity, if normal, to attachments to persons outside the family and of the opposite sex. Freud saw in primitive religions the confirmation of

Women, Adored and Abhorred 143

their sexual growth. Men first worship "Mother" Earth, the daedal source of being. After her, the great goddesses who represented her in man's affection and devotion, preceded in time the worship of sky gods. Then followed the Father God WKKO, an ancient sky god to whom the Finns prayed for rain. In Egypt, before Osiris, there was Amon-Ra, a sky god for whose honor the great temples at Karnak and Luxor were built. He was dethroned briefly by Aton, an even greater sky god, conceived in his spiritual greatness by King Ikhnaton. Aton is the source of all life, the force behind the sun, symbolized but not portrayed by the disc of the sun, from which rays ending in hands emerge. The hands again symbolically hold gifts for man. The sky gods, and their number was legion, were considered as father-gods. The worship of the father-gods eventually eclipsed the worship of the Great Mother, eclipsed but never eradicated it. Christian Science today has reinstated the mother-god worship in the hyphenated father-mother god to whom its prayers may be addressed.

The great emotional appeal which belief in a father-god has over the belief in an impersonal force was illustrated by the brief reign of Aton, a non-personal god brilliantly and nobly conceived by Ikhnaton. Although when he became king, Ikhnaton had tried to erase all visible signs of the father-god Amon-Ra who preceded Aton, no sooner was Ikhnaton himself dead than the worship of Amon-Ra returned and the worship of an impersonal creative force, though symbolized by the disc of the sun itself, disappeared from Egypt.

Certain aspects of life in modern Italy today would seem inexplicable to anyone quite innocent of Freudian explanations and unacquainted with the history of the religions of the world. In modern Italy, the cult of devotion to suffering and protecting womanhood is almost universal. Woman is on a pedestal, whether deified as *La Madonna* or sentimentally enshrined as Mamma Mia.

In a most readable book, *The Italians*, first printed in 1964 and reprinted several times since, Luigi Barzini notes that possibly as many churches in Italy are dedicated to the Madonna as to Christ and that to her belong the most revered and frequented shrines; that Italy abounds in miraculous images of her; and that most Italian men are under her direct protection, as "Maria" is usually one of the names given to a man-child at christening. It is also conceded that it is not uncommon in Italy for a man who expects his wife to be demurely devoted to him to think none the less of himself nor be less esteemed by his men friends or in some cases by his wife if it is known he has a mistress.

The ever-changing religious mores of marriage, whether viewed in historical or in contemporary perspective, inevitably reflect the status of women at the period in question. In primitive tribes, and this is true of primitive tribes today, marriage was and is a transaction not so much between husband and wife as between the chiefs of their respective clans or tribes. Its object was to prevent incest. Neither husband nor wife counted as individuals but only as tribesmen, and, as Freud showed in *Totem and Taboo*, the exogamy enforced by marriage taboos had reference to totem bonds, rather than bloodlines. Contemporary society tends to reverse this practice. It looks dubiously on marriages of mixed faiths because it thinks the individual husband's and wife's happiness will be in jeopardy, not because one faith group or the other is threatened.

Wherever and whenever a woman could be taken as a wife as part of the spoils of battle or by purchase and counted as part of her husband's wealth, a virtual slave without rights or redress, there was usually no marriage ceremony civil or religious, just possession. However, cohabitation acquired dignity for the wife as well as the husband when in ancient Greece, or in Rome from later republican times on, marriage was possible without any ceremony, civil or religious, and was entirely in the hands of the two parties to the union. They had the right to terminate it as easily and as simply, for it was regarded as a personal matter. Not until the fourth century in Rome was the Christian dogma of the sacramental nature of marriage recognized.

It was St. Augustine who made clear the threefold obligations of a married pair to each other, to their offspring, and to God. The indissolubility of marriage was a debatable idea in the church until about A.D. 900, and always its sacrosanct nature has been

Women, Adored and Abhorred

violated by attitudes of indulgence toward unfaithfulness by the husband, tolerance of prostitution, and an almost tender consideration of mistresses. The utter contempt the world felt for an unfaithful wife, a religious abhorrence, contrasted strangely with the common acceptance of a glamorous mistress.

In Christian countries it was not until 1563, after the Council of Trent, that church law required the celebration of a marriage before the parish priest or local ordinary and two witnesses. Before 1563 the priest could meet the lovers outside the church doors, bless them, and depart. If they then promised each other to live as man and wife and consummated that promise, they were married without possibility of divorce. In Scotland, informal marriage was possible until 1939, and in the United States, even in the second half of the twentieth century, common-law marriage, the quintessence of informality, is recognized as binding in 18 of the 50 states.

Lord Hardwicke led the reform of marriage laws in England in 1753 to make them conform with the marriage rites of the Church of England. The church forbade the marriage of cousins as incestuous and added another interdiction strangely like totem-relatedness, which seems to many people a fantastic limitation on marriage. It was the concept of "affinity," which has to do with marrying, for instance, a deceased wife's sister." It has been pointed out that if Henry VIII had not wished to seek papal dispensation for annulling his marriage to Catherine of Aragon, it could have been declared null and void on the grounds of affinity, as Catherine was his hapless brother Arthur's widow.

Before the eighteenth century, marriage was strictly a religious affair in the various countries of Europe. Today in many parts of the world, as in the Soviet Union, it is strictly a civil matter. In others, as usually in the United States, it is regarded as both a legal contract and a sacrament. The French Revolution established civil marriage in France; Bismarck established it in Germany. In only a few parts of Europe is a compulsory religious ceremony essential—notably in Greece and Vatican City—and in Israel for a Jew.

In vast areas of Asia, where the concept of the large family prevails, embracing uncles, aunts and cousins, authority is in the hands of its elders. The selection of marriage partners is left in the wise hands of those elders. For young people to fall in love before marriage is a form of juvenile delinquency, firmly overruled. If young people fall in love after marriage, well and good, but not before. Marriage is a concern of the family group as it is designed to prolong the group through offspring, and to insure their protection and nurture while young. If a man doesn't happen to fancy the wife chosen for him, or the wife the husband, it's just too bad, but like hard work and taxes must be accepted. This bears less heavily on a Moslem husband than on those of most other faiths, for if he can afford them, he may have as many as four wives, if he will promise to treat them equally. Among the four there is always the happy chance there may be one who is congenial. But the wife must put up with one husband, for in many parts of the world her wishes, even with respect to the fathering of the children she is expected to bear, do not count for much.

In most aboriginal tribes, even today, prenuptial intercourse is not merely condoned, it is expected. The temporary unions are, however, hedged about with barriers against incest, strict observance of exogamy, and in some cases other local restrictions. The Trobriand Islanders are an outstanding example. However, it is understood that the offspring of such premarital intercourse must be destroyed at birth, as illegitimacy is not allowed.

St. Paul is credited with introducing into Christianity the idea that marriage is a sacrament. In that famous and earnest letter he wrote to the Ephesians, realist and at the same time mystic that he was, he first deplored the "lusts of the flesh" that beset man and then recognized the state of marriage and sought to lift it to a harmonious beauty consonant with pure religion. He sought to remove all bickering and disharmony from marriage by enjoining wives to be obedient to their husbands in all things (there was no doubt in his mind who was in command). He sought to elevate and sanctify the relationship by comparing the relationship of wife and husband with the mystic union of the church with Christ. He wrote: "but as the church is subject to

Women, Adored and Abhorred

Christ so let the wives also be to their husbands in everything. . . . He that loveth his own wife loveth himself. . . . For this cause shall a man leave his father and mother and shall cleave to his wife: and the twain shall become one flesh. This mystery is great, but I speak in regard of Christ and the church."

To compare the intercourse of a man with his wife with the union of Christ and his church is a startling idea. Indeed, it is a distorted and exaggerated simile which can be assessed psychologically as overcompensation. From his other statements about sexual union we know the idea was abhorrent to St. Paul and that he regarded the married state as a necessary evil for a man not strong enough and not pure enough to remain celibate.

In his intense love for the little group of Christians at Ephesus, and with a realistic appraisal of the social scene, Paul did what he could and in the only way natural to him to raise marriage to a spiritual level. He gave it deep religious meaning.

It is doubtful that a figure of speech ever really hallowed anything, and in the case of St. Paul, considering his other utterances on sexual desire, it may not have been efficacious even in his own mind. What the church sanctioned and blessed in marriage in St. Paul's letter to the good people of Ephesus, and what the church sanctions and blesses today in the ritual for the solemnization of matrimony in the Book of Common Prayer and in the ritual of Rome and the many other rituals patterned upon them, is the cohabitation of a man and woman "according to God's holy ordinances." We know today that this physical aspect of marriage is only part and a strangely brittle part of marriage. Without psychological, as well as physical bonds of marriage, the period between the wedding day and the granting of a final decree of divorce is often brief.

The physical attraction so frequently mistaken for love and often leading to a precipitate marriage is not at all the same thing as the love which really hallows marriage. Erich Fromm in his book *The Art of Love*, which has been translated into 17 languages and read in printing after printing the world over, says that most people think of love in a passive way, as being loved, and not as an activity, namely loving, calling for maturity, self-knowledge, self-respect, and courage. He uses the old myth of Adam and Eve in a masterly way to make clear his meaning. He says that after Adam and Eve had eaten "of the tree of knowledge of good and evil," that is, after their recognition of themselves as human beings of different sexes, "they saw that they were naked and were ashamed." They were ashamed because they saw they were different and separate and although there had been physical union, there was as yet no psychological union; that is clear, Fromm says, because Adam tried to defend himself by blaming Eve when God questioned him. Had he been joined to Eve by love, he would have defended her and felt no shame, no guilt.

A new marriage ceremony remains to be written that will make husband and wife aware not only of what it is to be of one flesh, but of one mind, one purpose, one life. The art of loving, like the art of living or the art of music, must be learned. Too many of us react to "loving" and "living" as we do to music and wonder why we fail to enjoy any of them. We remain passive and expect "loving" to flow over us like music, or life to flow past us like sound. That is not to love, or to live, any more than it is to hear music. As many people hear sounds but not music, because they are ignorant of its art, so many never love because they do not know that to love in more than an infantile fashion takes study and hard work, self-discipline and great objectivity. When a person has mastered the art of loving in a mature fashion, then as St. Paul said, "love seeketh not its own, is not provoked, taketh not account of evil. . . . love never faileth."

Unfortunately, the days immediately preceding a modern wedding and the day itself are not days of instruction in loving. Worse still, they are usually for the bride a retreat into infantile love of herself. She becomes what a baby is, the contented center of adulation and care. "All the best shops" have lists of the patterns she wants in silver, crystal and china. As a bride-to-be she is queen at showers, teas, dances, receptions, and dinners. She acquires a truly royal trousseau and sometimes the illusion that life will be like this from now on. On her wedding day, the ceremony becomes an elaborate theatrical production for which rehearsals are necessary. The climax of the drama is not the usually inaudible exchange of vows for which the principal actors appear not to know their parts, but must be prompted for every phrase. It is the dramatic moment of a wedding when, heralded by music, the entire congregation stands and turns to stare at the bride as she stands ready to march down the long central aisle on her father's arm. She may not walk with natural grace, but must feign a halting reluctance, as in a fashion show when the lovely models know they are visions of delight.

After the ceremony there follows an inexorable order of events: first, a long wait to secure photographs to publicize the production, then the bride and groom emerging from the church doors, ducking the rice and its symbolism; the reception with all and sundry indiscriminately privileged to kiss the bride; then the further playacting of cake-cutting, removing the bride's garter, throwing away her bouquet, much as Miss America relinquishes her crown.

Unfortunately, a modern wedding usually gives free reign to all the vulgar, mercenary, superficial attitudes toward marriage current in our day. But as Eleanore Wembridge wrote in 1939 in *Life Among the Lowbrows*, when morons wed, "if the veil is long enough, enough jokes are made by the best man, and enough shrieks uttered by the bridesmaids, the impression is made on the dimly endowed pair that something really important socially has taken place."

However much morons may still need such a wedding, it is a question how much longer this mode will go unchallenged by essentially thoughtful and honest young people today. They have shown they are not awed by tradition. The Haight-Ashbury revolt of the flower-children is not the alternative. They, like most rebels, are romanticists. Like Rousseau, they would revert to the primitive as the natural. They are unaware that the "noble savage" whom they and other sentimentalists idealize, has never existed. Slowly, very slowly, man has been climbing up to decency. Only rarely, even now, does he manage truly to love another as himself. The wise know that loving is not immersion in a nebulous, drug-induced dream, flooded by rosy light, but is a strenuous, often heart-breaking endeavor, and that to love truly and maturely is one of the sternest commands of life.

CHAPTER XIV

"Mirror, Mirror, Tell Me True"

In the wise old fairy tale, the mirror on the wall replied that the Queen was fair, but her rival, her step-daughter, was fairer far. This the jealous Queen could not brook, although the mirror assured her that her own beauty was undiminished. To be surpassed was intolerable.

In a measure the fairy tale can be applied to the strange rivalry between religion and ethics. Devout writers of a variety of faiths unite to say that ethics is the fair daughter of religion but are quick to add that moral conduct must not be taken as a substitute for faith, which is the essence of religion. To know the "truth" is more important for salvation than to be good. Though "thy sins be as scarlet," acceptance of the "truth" can wash them "whiter than snow."

The mooted hierarchy of values is a persistent philosophical question, as well as one which vexes rival religions. There are great religions, such as Confucianism and Buddhism, which hold that ethical values are supreme. Indeed, some more radical branches of Christian Protestant faith, such as Unitarianism and the Ethical Science movement, elevate the values that emanate from feelings of human brotherhood to first place. They consider them above and indeed independent in origin from the matters of faith. But, not so, maintains the typical, sturdily orthodox Christian. The value of faith is supreme. It is his contention that without faith true morality is impossible as he believes it is loving obedience to God's will, not a human achievement in interpersonal living.

The written testimony of the great religions of the world with their remarkable agreement upon man's central duty in life makes clear the hollowness of this contention, as certain of these religions explicitly deny the existence of a personal God with a declared "will." Consider the following "Golden Rules:" Buddhism says: "Hurt not others with that which pains yourself (Udanavarga). Hinduism: "This is the sum of duty: do naught to others which if done to thee would cause thee pain" (Mahabbarata). Zoroastrianism has this injunction: "That nature only is good when it will not do to another whatever is not good for its own self" (Dadistan—1 dinki). In the Analects of Confucius we read: "Is there any one maxim which ought to be acted upon throughout one's whole life? Surely the maxim of loving-kindness is such—Do not unto others what you would not they should do unto you." Taoists are taught: "Regard your neighbor's gain as your own gain; regard your neighbor's loss as your own loss" (Tai Shang Kan Ying P'ien).

The Hebrews are instructed in the Talmud: "What is hurtful to yourself do not to your fellow man. That is the whole of the Torah and the remainder is but commentary. Go learn it." Islam in its traditions insists on the oneness of brotherly love and faith: "No one of you is a believer until he loves for his brother what he loves for himself." Jainism is explicit in saying: "In happiness and suffering, in joy and grief, we should regard all creatures as we regard our own self, and should therefore refrain from inflicting upon others such injury as would appear undesirable to us if inflicted upon ourselves" (Yogashastra). In this central teaching the Jainists extend the application of the Golden Rule to all living creatures, even ants and angleworms. Sikism makes salvation depend on morality: "As thou deemest thyself so deem others. Then shalt thou become a partner in heaven" (Kabir). As Christians we are familiar with the statement of the law in the New Testament as written in Matthew: "All things whatsoever ye would that men should do to you, do ye even so to them for this is the law and the prophets."

Yet for the Islamic world, as well as for orthodox Christians, and in part for Jews, faith, the adherence to a definite creed, is the essence of religion. The consequence is that they have no choice but to be bigots. For them, the unbeliever, the infidel, the adherent to a different creed, no matter what his moral merit, is a lost soul who has forfeited salvation. Disbelief is religious treason.

"True believers," no matter what the creed to which they are committed, are strangely unmoved concerning the correctness of their convictions by the evidence produced by modern scholarship. This evidence makes clear that pantheon after pantheon has been created to satisfy man's needs, his fears, his hopes. Such true believers view the historical record of the procession of the gods, who faded into oblivion when they failed to satisfy their creators with no sense of relevance, but those gods "were mere myths," they say, and have no likeness to "our God."

Like Canon Grensted in the Brampton lectures for 1930 at Oxford, they say that, of course, nothing could save the gods of Olympus from oblivion, for with all their beauty, they had no more reality than the emotions from which they sprang. And, with Canon Grensted, they ask, who wants to save them anyway, "or any of the gods of the nations?"

Serenely secure in the fortress of his true belief, each Christian, each Jew, each Moslem, each devotee of Siva, holds fast to the one reality he has grasped, his god, who is the one true god. He should. To be steadfastly loyal to the truth as he sees it is a man's obligation. Therein lies honor and uprightness. However, only when a man knows that such truth itself may change, may grow, is his loyalty safe from becoming fanaticism. It was said of John Stuart Mill that he had a mind open to new truths, no matter how disconcerting to his previous convictions. To have convictions and at the same time an open mind qualified him to belong to the Socratic household.

In the end, we must come to terms with a philosophical question: Is there one or are there two ways of knowing? Do we reach religious truth, as scientists do, through experimental probing of the given facts, careful observation, cautious classification, and logical exactness in deduction and in formulation of hypotheses? Does the religious thinker test his hypotheses, namely his creeds, and discard a creed for a better one? Is there one and only one way open to the scientist seeking "truth," and is there an additional way open to the seer, the prophet, the imam seeking religious truth?

The great German philosopher Immanuel Kant answered the question in a manner which many people find acceptable. He demonstrated, ponderously, but lucidly and definitively, that whenever we try to establish a truth that transcends our experience, even though we employ the most strict scientific reasoning, we end in contradictions. Take for instance the problems: Had time a beginning? Or, is space infinite? Does God exist? Using the facts we have, we can establish with equal logic both the affirmative and negative conclusions to these questions. Kant called these contradictions "antinomies." The fact that one logically proved truth cancels out the direct opposite, which is equally correct logically, shows that neither conclusion is correct and further that we cannot reach certainty by reasoning when we go beyond facts of experience.

But Kant was deeply aware of man's wish, indeed of his need, to project his certainty beyond his experience. He argued that man is a citizen of two worlds—the world he explores through his senses and his intellect, the world of pure experience which we usually call the world of science, and another, the transcendental world, a world where profound and meaningful mysteries such as immortality, infinity, and deity lurk. Kant thought we could reach certainty by intuition—not reason—on some aspects of the transcendental world, where, he said, we are also citizens. Psychologically, intuition as he used it is based on two native human traits, man's ability to feel "awe" and to experience a feeling of "ought." The aesthetic experience of awe inspired by "the starry heavens above" creates in us the humility that points to the existence of infinite greatness, while the ethical feeling of obligation in conduct, an obligation transcending all legal demands or humanly derived norms of behavior, proclaims us free citizens in a world that transcends this world of experience with its strictures.

Thus Kant has concluded that mankind has two separate and distinct avenues to certainty and that he uses reason or the intellect when he wishes to reach truth in the world of science but with equal justification depends on intuition when he must be certain about transcendental matters.

Too often we overlook the difference between the truth or certainty arrived at by intellectual processes and "revealed truth," akin to Rousseau's *bonne foi*, the product of intuition. The "truth" of scientific effort continues to grow as we gather more data; the revealed truth is a finished product when delivered to us in a flash.

This vital difference, the ambitious religious movement known as Bahaism has unfortunately overlooked. Bahaism looks confidently for the ultimate union of all religion. Overlooking the diamond-like resistance to change of the various religious creeds, it notes, correctly, the unanimity with which world religions enshrine the concept of human brotherhood at the very center of their ethical teaching. Not Jesus only, but Moses, Mohammed, Buddha, Confucius, Zoroaster, Mahavira, the great religious leaders of the ages have proclaimed their wording of the Golden Rule time and again. It is conceivable that the great religions of the world in some happier future, working perhaps through the United Nations, may produce a Constitution for the world with a preamble based on the solemn recognition of human brotherhood.

But this will not remove the difficulties in the way of Bahaism's dream of uniting all religions. The transcendental beliefs on which the religions rest, being matters of faith built on "revealed truths" are resistant to change. They are not malleable. They can be shattered but not shaped.

On the part of a believer, tolerance of the slightest deviation from revealed truth is equivalent to disbelief. It is disloyalty. Nothing so sharply delineates the difference between truth arrived at by scientific method and truth reached by intuition or revelation as the proneness of the intellectual truth to change, grow, develop, while mystics' truth upheld by emotional conviction does not alter. It is absolute and immutable. As it cannot be proved, neither can it be disproved. Sometimes, when the emotional conviction which supports it crumbles, it is forgotten. Sometimes a new revelation with more prestige topples it.

"Mirror, Mirror, Tell Me True"

Bahaism, first introduced into North America in 1890 and claiming today a membership of many thousands, is too significant a movement to be dismissed with the blank assertion that its main goal is unattainable. It is a brave example of an attempt to subordinate belief to ethical conduct in the hierarchy of values by uniting Moslems and Christians in a declaration that acting in accordance with the principle of brotherly love is the prime requisite for salvation.

In 1844, Mirza Ali Mohammed of Shiraz founded an Islamic sect of which he became the leader or Bab. The Arabic word "Bab" means "gate," and in assuming the title, Mirza assumed the role of prophet or gateway for revealed truth. One of the two rival Islamic sects, the Shirtes, believes that their last great leader, their Imam, became invisible in 874 A.D. but will return "at the end of time" to establish justice on earth. In the meantime, his will is made known to them by a succession of "Babs."

Mirza was not long content to be a mere Bab and declared himself the expected "Imam." He had zealous followers, but even stronger opponents, for the role of Imam had political implications, too, and the Turkish government had him executed in 1850. The religious strife did not, however, end with his execution, and hostilities for the role of "Bab" broke out between two half brothers. Again the Turkish government acted to prevent civil as well as religious strife and banished one to Cyprus and the other to Haifa, Israel. The "Bab" in Israel, Baha-i-ullah—a vigorous missionary spirit—extended the teaching of "Babism" abroad. At first Baha-i-ullah spread the faith almost exclusively in Iran. His grandson Shoghi Effendi Robbani, Defender of the Faith, outdid his grandfather in missionary zeal and continued to extend the now worldwide community of Babism of which he was the spiritual head until his death in 1957. It was renamed Bahaism in honor of Shoghi Effendi Robanni's grandfather, Baha-i-ullah.

This religion, although not introduced to the Western World until 1890, by 1920 had taken such strong hold that its main temple was built on the shore of Lake Michigan at Wilmette, Illinois. Its beautiful Levant architecture, strange to western eyes unaccustomed to onion domes against the sky, caused the temple to be nicknamed "God's lemon squeezer," but in spite of such irreverences, the faith has spread widely.

The Bahai doctrine is that God is essentially unknowable, but that aspects of his divinity have been and will be made manifest to meet the needs of humanity from time to time. Such manifestations in the past have been made through Abraham, Zoroaster, Jesus, Buddha, and of course Mohammed. The sacred literature of the Bahai faith consists of the Koran and the writings and spoken words of their Babs.

There are cogent reasons for its wide and easy acceptance in the United States, a non-Moslem country. Men like its tolerance. Every religion, it insists, has at least a partial glimpse of the truth about the one God, and all religions accept the ethics of human brotherhood. In addition, Bahaism is an optimistic religion. It claims that the study of the religions of the world shows there is a progressive, divine plan for the education of the race. God, the great schoolmaster, is patient, knowing graduation day is not yet, although it is approaching. Finally, there is no priesthood and no ritual of worship, but there is leadership.

The Arabic word for leader is "imam," which signifies leader in the meaning of a pattern to be followed, an exemplar. In the Koran, God, speaking to Abraham says: "Lo I make thee an imam for mankind." Hence the head of a Moslem community is an imam. The two opposing Islamic sects differ concerning the appointment of an imam. The Sunnites hold an imam is chosen by his fellowmen, but the Shirtes, in general, believe an imam is God-elected and that he is both infallible and free from possibility of sin. The concept should not be difficult for either Protestants or Catholics to grasp as in many ways Imam is equivalent to Pope.

Strangely enough for the orthodox in Islam and in Christianity, their very agreement about the concept of sin creates an insurmountable barrier to the union in one faith for which Bahaism hopes. We often ignore the fact that the word "sin" has stronger religious than ethical implications. It has to do essentially with a creature's relation to his creator and only incidentally with his relations with his fellowmen. It means aliena-

"Mirror, Mirror, Tell Me True"

tion from God, or Allah—through lack of faith, often manifesting itself in lack of obedience. It is breaking the First Commandment. Bahaism considers it tolerance for a Christian to worship Allah as prescribed in the Koran and for a Moslem to accept the triune God as presented in the Bible as "the one God." But a true believer in either faith would know that to do so would be to commit sin.

As one can admit the equality of religious beliefs as different insights about the nature of deity only by a denial of the rightful supremacy of the creed about "the one true God" as revealed in one's own religion, such tolerance cannot be less than sinful heresy. Revealed truth, by its nature, as given rather than put together by hard labor over a period of time, is immutable, "the same, yesterday, today and forever."

In passing, it is worthy of note that the interpretaion of sin as alienation from God, or disloyalty to him, solves a great mystery. It explains how a deathbed repentance and renewal of faith can wipe out sin. Although the dying man's heart may still be full of malice toward his fellowmen, if he believes there exists a god powerful enough to admit him to heaven, he will possess the Open Sesame to bliss. This, for those who esteem faith as the essential for salvation, is orthodoxy.

At this point we must consider Theosophy or, as its followers call it, "The Ancient Wisdom." It, too, is an attempt to unite an Eastern and a Western religion. It is an amalgam of Hinduism and Christianity which, according to its founder, Mrs. Annie Besant, an Englishwoman, long resident in India, aims by purging both religions of the superstitious myths which have encrusted them to reveal their essential unity. According to Theosophy, there is one Divine Reality, called Brahma by Hindus and God by Christians. Emerson called it "The Oversoul." Other American transcendentalists accepted the idea of a World Soul, among them Thoreau, who with Hindu teaching helped form the mind of Gandhi. Theosophists take from Hindu teaching the law of Karma, not too difficult for a Western mind to accept as the law of cause and effect. Two other Hindu beliefs incorporated in the teaching of Theosophy, namely, the doctrines of the cyclic rhythm of the universe and reincarnation, are further from Western modes of thought. Yet without undue strain and distortion, these seemingly alien ways of viewing progress may be viewed as a single way, as in a stanza written by Conrad Aiken from an evolutionary point of view. The stanza occurs in *Senlin, a Biography*.

> Or was I, the single ant, or tinier thing,
> That crept from rocks of buried time.
> And dedicated its holy life to climb
> From atom to beetling atom, jagged grain to grain
> Patiently and out of the darkness, we call sleep
> Into the hollow gigantic world of light
> Thinking the sky to be its destined shell,
> Hoping to fit it well!

Even as aspiring life never does exactly fit the hollow shell of the sky it hopes to fill, so the aim of fitting Hinduism and Christianity into a common mold, the shell of Theosophy, is doomed to failure. Each has its revealed truths, and jagged granite resists squeezing.

Although not all Christians stake their hope of salvation on the act of faith alone, evangelical Protestantism most frequently challenges the law of cause and effect. It teaches that in this wicked world, this "World Aflame," belief can bring instant divine forgiveness to stand between a wicked man and his just punishment. It was quite differently that the great Catholic poet Dante portrayed the scheme of redemption in the *Divine Comedy*. He wrote sternly and inexorably of divine justice rather than divine forgiveness. Every punishment in purgatory fitted the crime—was, indeed, an outgrowth and logical consequence of it. With all pretense stripped away, each soul in purgatory or paradise lived as it really was. It was not a vindictive verdict which the poet thought God imposed on man for his misbehavior. Man endured what he had earned, the ineluctable justice of cause and effect. But as Dante viewed his fellowmen as inclined to avarice, deceit, cruelty, and lechery, his picture of life after death is grim.

"Mirror, Mirror, Tell Me True"

Confession, penance, absolution, all have to do with moral bookkeeping, not with faith. Indeed, when one comes to the concept of indulgences, as Luther saw, the bookkeeping tends to deviate from the strict rule of justice. He saw clearly that either the priests of the church lied or God could be bribed.

There are many persons, well known to history, who might be selected as fitting examples of men of highest moral worth who have been martyred for their faith, or lack of faith. Spinoza was such a man, and I select him because during his life he was anathematized as an atheist, while later centuries have hailed him as the "God-intoxicated philosopher."

The year 1632, Spinoza's birth year, seems long ago, but actually it was yesterday in the history of mankind, and the tragedy of Spinoza's life ordeal is a present tragedy in the world. Benedictus Spinoza, or Baruch de Espinoza, as he was known to his fellow exiled Spanish Jews in Amsterdam, was a youth of excellent promise. The elders of the synagogue, impressed by his brilliant mind, offered him an annuity, for he was very poor, if he would renounce the heresy to which much reading of philosophy and much thinking had brought him. This he could not do. He could not accept, as adequate, the conception of a God who favored a particular people. Such a god would be limited, not infinite. Spinoza spoke of the necessity for men to put first in their lives "the intellectual love of God," but he considered it preposterous that God should, or could, love man in return. God might have a body—the vast limitless world of matter that fills the void—for as infinite, God must be the "All-that-is," and through science, we reverently approach fragmentary glimpses of the orderly impersonality of "The All."

For this belief, the Ecclesiastical Council pronounced upon Spinoza the following Anathema which I quote from Durant's *Story of Philosophy*, as translated by Willis and reported by Van Vloten:

> With the judgment of the angels and the sentence of the saints, we anathematize, execrate, curse, and cast out Baruch de Espinoza, the whole of the sacred community assenting, in the presence of the sacred books with the six-hundred-and-

thirteen precepts written therein, pronouncing against him the malediction wherewith Elisha cursed the children, and all the maledictions written in the Book of the Law. Let him be accursed by day, and accursed by night, let him be accursed in his lying down, and accursed in his rising up, accursed in going out and accursed in coming in—May the Lord never more pardon or acknowledge him; may the wrath and displeasure of the Lord burn henceforth against this man, load him with all the curses written in the Book of the Law, and blot out his name from under the sky; may the Lord sever him for ever from all the tribes of Israel, weight him with all the maledictions of the firmament contained in the Book of Law; and may all ye who are obedient to the Lord your God be saved this day.

Hereby then are all admonished that none hold converse with him by word of mouth. None hold communication with him by writing; that no one do him any service, no one abide under the same roof with him, no one approach within four cubits length of him, and no one read any document dictated by him, or written by his hand.

The malediction worked, heeded at least by his co-religionists, though perhaps not by the Deity, considering Spinoza's posthumous fame and his common description as the "God-intoxicated philosopher." He was sheltered by some Dutch Protestant friends and supported himself in an attic, by grinding lenses. He died beloved by a few friends for his gentle, kindly ways and left to the world his incomparable philosophical treatises, his *Ethics*.

In the fairy tale, the vain Queen attempted to destroy her step-daughter when the mirror said that she was fairer than the Queen. This reminds me that Canon Grensted puts Confucianism and Buddhism in their place as not really religions because they put foremost in importance man's search for a correct way of life, not his devotion to God. In spite of the vast numbers who have adhered and do adhere to their teachings, they are just not

"Mirror, Mirror, Tell Me True"

religions, according to the Canon. Was William James right or wrong when he defined religion as man's gift of the best he has to the highest he knows? Or is Otto more nearly right when he defines religion as an attitude toward "the holy" which must have in it something of mystery and awe?

Buddha had no wish to be called a god. He wanted to be known as "the enlightened one," and his contribution to the world in the religion which bears his name (pace Canon Grensted!) is, as the Canon says, a plan for salvation in this life. Buddha remade Hinduism by ignoring its transcendental beliefs. He wanted to teach men how to be happy. He was indeed pragmatic. He was also profound.

The insight or intuition which came to the Buddha as he sat meditating under the bo tree in the Deer Park near Benares was not born of a faculty distinct from and superceding reason. It was the culmination of reasoning, the sudden clarification anyone experiences as a chaotic puzzle suddenly assumes form. He grasped the meaning of life. Simply, clearly, and with assurance Buddha enunciated an ethical pattern for living, which he promised could bring happiness. Millions through the centuries have accepted his Four Noble Truths and essayed to follow in the Eightfold Path. Later followers added a creed, made Buddha a god, not content with the teacher they had, and introduced the subtleties of transcendental ideas for priests to puzzle over and followers to stumble over.

Considering the rivalry between ethics and faith, each called the essence of religion, it would be an historical oversight to omit consideration of Auguste Comte's Religion of Humanity. In it, the great positivist philosopher tried to reconcile faith and ethics. He was born in Montpelier, France, in 1798, and the five volumes of his *Positive Philosophy* appeared between 1830 and 1842. His influence spread far beyond France and won him such distinguished adherents in England as the two Mills, James and John Stuart, Alexander Bain, psychologist and moralist, and George Henry Lewis.

Comte's positivism was a philosophy dominated by what he called the Law of Three Stages. At first, he said, mankind explained natural events in a theological fashion. Sunrise, for instance, was the return of a god. Sickness was caused by the anger of a god. The second stage, Comte called the metaphysical. Here explanation was considered adequate only if some abstract concept could be found into which the particular problem under discussion could be fitted. Thus, stars moved in circles because circles were the most perfect figure. But in Comte's day he held that science was coming into its own, and he taught that explanation of all problems from astronomical to sociological must follow the positive method of science, which implies precise observation and hypotheses tested by experimentation. The underlying assumption is the regularity of cause and effect.

When he came to consider religion, Comte found the concept of God to be a metaphysical abstraction and concluded that the real object of man's devotion should be no less than humanity itself—Past, Present, and Future. He devised ceremonial worship of humanity, with rites, prayers and discipline. He even devised a new Judgment Day.

The plan for Judgment Day à la Positivism was as follows: A certain number of years after a man's death, when emotional prejudices about him had had time to fade, a panel of his peers was to evaluate the worth of each man's life, and vote whether his name was worthy to be inscribed on the great scroll of humanity, along with the names of others who during their lifetime had contributed something to be remembered and treasured.

This inspired George Eliot, herself a Positivist, to write the "Choir Invisible," a noble and much loved poem which reads:

> O may I join the choir invisible
> Of these immortal dead who live again
> In minds made better by their presence
>   O may I join the choir invisible
>   May I reach
>   That purest heaven, be to other souls
>   The cup of strength in some great agony.

Comte's "Religion of Humanity" did not become a vital religion. Mention of it today in a class in the history of philosophy serves usually as a moment of amused relaxation at the vagaries of a once great thinker in his decline. Yet positivism, though no longer the force it was, still exerts an influence in contemporary thought and especially in contemporary religious thought. S. Alexander, a modern realist, who wrote *Space, Time, and Deity*, conceives of Deity as an emergence. He views reality as a vast pyramid resting on the base of space, which was devoid of life, motion change, but from which emerged the level of time, characterized by movement, change, and the long eons during which ever more complicated forms of life emerged. The emergence of consciousness ushered in the final level, which he calls Deity. This level even now is moving toward an evolution of values of supreme and infinite worth, which will constitute that Deity toward which man reverently but stumblingly moves. In this concept there is no room for rivalry of ethical and religious values, only a hope for their progressive growth. But how many have taken time to read Professor Alexander's *Space, Time and Deity*, or even know that it exists?

In the meantime, the name of another religion, Zen Buddhism, is on many men's tongues, particularly young peoples', and it solves the problem by never raising the issue between believing and behaving as rival paths to salvation. It offers satisfying samples of salvation first and lets believing and behaving flow from that experience.

Too few people realize the hidden ways in which the persistent problem of salvation through faith or through works still confuses mankind and increases the nameless, free-floating anxiety which bedevils man and has been called the dominant curse of our society. Most people conceal the conflict even from themselves by a verbal formula to the effect that they know that "all the good will enjoy everlasting life"—and "good" in turn means observing the Golden Rule and accepting the creed of the particular religion to which they belong.

Really devout people do not question the correctness of the creed of the particular religions they adopt for several reasons. For one thing, they involve themselves totally in their own religious group. The more devout they are, the more they find themselves expected to expend themselves not in worship, but in supporting worship. Thy assume financial burdens—money is to be raised for salaries, maintenance, and building programs. There are social service programs of vast philanthropic and educational scope to be staffed and furthered. They are enmeshed in the proliferation of religious duties.

There is another reason why a creed is more commonly accepted than questioned. Strong emotion sanctions critical laziness in thinking in this sensitive area of life. "Faith of our fathers, holy faith," sounds comfortable, safe, and tenderly respectful to our parents' memory, as they gave it to us with our mother-tongue. Besides, the words theologians use in regard to matters of faith have vague connotations for many who hear them. Does transcendental truth, for instance, have something to do with outer space? Maybe whether science fiction is true? Few can really define it.

Yet, even the most orthodox and unquestioning parents become uneasy when their growing children press them for answers they cannot give. And the young, today, have an uncomfortable way of refusing to be put off with conventional replies. In this century of mass media of communication, children often have more knowledge of facts than their parents, thought not necessarily more wisdom. The healthful questioning of youth can easily be turned into rebellion.

The upshot is anxiety on both sides; the parents are anxious because they are insecure—insecure of their facts and insecure of their authority. The children are anxious because the parental authority upon which they have been accustomed to lean, has suddenly given way. Their crutch is gone. And in their baffled dismay they angrily reject all authority.

Into this gap in credibility and growing anxiety, Zen Buddhism, a religion new to the Western world, but ancient in the East, has stepped with quiet assurance and is gaining followers by the thousands. Zen Buddhism is Buddhism mellowed and enriched by long contact with Confucianism and Taoism. It does not, like Theosophy or Bahaism, seek to merge Oriental faiths with Christianity around a common accord on moral values, although that accord is there.

Instead, Zen's command is for a stern disregard of past convictions. "Empty your mind," says the Zen teacher. "What you think you know you know only in terms of words. Words deceive you. Tell me: Who are you? You can't give me a real answer? No, of course not. You don't really know. . . . Answer me this: You can make the sound of two hands clapping. Now what is the sound of one hand clapping?"

Undoubtedly the riddles or "Koans" with which Zen masters break down the new pupil's conviction that he is a knowledgeable person also make an unfair use of words, but they do accomplish their mission and forcibly reinforce the command to empty the mind.

It is without doubt a relief to empty one's mind, for students report that with that act, too, go the anxieties engendered by unresolved contradictions, the driving restlessness of the feeling of unfinished business, the aggressive assertiveness born of frustration. They are replaced by a sense of the power that comes with yielding. It is the same relaxed strength exemplified in the Zen physical skill of Judo, of Zen paintings of snow-laden branches that, because they bend easily, lose their burden and do not break. It is the "Nowness" of Zen ceremonial tea hours, which shut out past and future to arrest and enjoy the transcendent beauty of the uneventful "Now." It is the preponderance of unused space in Zen pictorial art, which dominates and seems important to the extent that the few painted details are merely illustrations of it. It is unbroken "Oneness," which is the wordless creed of Zen.

Zen Buddhism permits no questioning of the mirror on the wall. It says instead: Look directly at a single flower or the curve of a hill against the sky. Sit relaxed and look, really look at what is. Then you tell me, "What God and man is."

CHAPTER XV

Twin Sisters

The experience of the sublime stubbornly defies exact classification in spite of Edmund Burke's treatise on the subject. There is in it an awe-engendering submissiveness which is religious. There is an exultation which is esthetic. It is, like religion, quite often an affirmation of something that strains credulity. This may be what Tom Paine saw in it when, in *The Age of Reason* he wrote that "it (sublimity) borders on the ridiculous." It is also quite as often "the perfect embodiment" of "meaning in form," which the philosopher Bosanquet defined as beauty.

In experiences less than sublime, the twin sisters, the experience of holiness and the experience of beauty, often are found together. They are easily mistaken for each other. A friend, daughter of a Congregational minister who had lived as a child in a small Connecticut town, told me one day that central heating and modern plumbing had destroyed her capacity for religious ecstasy. The parsonage of her childhood had neither central heating nor running water. She had a Saturday night bath in a portable tin bathtub on a bench beside the kitchen range. The following Sunday morning, sitting in the minister's pew, her small body still delightfully refreshed from the bath, wearing her spotless Sunday dress, her fresh undergarments faintly lavender-scented from the clothes-press, she regularly experienced heavenly bliss. She heard her father's beloved voice in the long prayer asking God's blessing on each member of the congregation, and she mounted with it into the very presence of God to experience his beatitude. Now, she said, with a daily shower and drip-dry lingerie and frocks fresh each morning, she goes to church but has no ecstasy. She is usually critical of the sermon and dreads the responsive reading as an ordeal of voices out of step.

It is obvious that we frequently mistake various emotional

Twin Sisters

attitudes for something other than they are. Hurt pride can masquerade as righteous indignation; greed can be "standing up for one's rights"; conceit as proper self-respect is all too common. When we exact "an eye for an eye, a tooth for a tooth," what we call justice may look to the world like vengeance. But there are no attitudes we are more apt to confuse than the religious and the esthetic.

The twenty-ninth Psalm exhorts us to worship God "in the beauty of holiness," thus connecting beauty with holiness as its fragrance is connected with a flower. When a perfumer, reversing nature's procedure, destroys flowers to extract their fragrance, full half of what we prize in the resulting essence is the suggestion it brings of uncrushed flowers. Part of an experience tends to reinstate a former delightful whole. The odor of pine needles, as we enter a room on a winter's day, can conjure up a pine-clothed mountain slope in full summer sun. In like manner, the act of worship the world over has commonly welded the attitude of reverence so firmly into the structure of beauty that we fail to distinguish them. They assist each other. Each is augmented by the other. Either can arrest a man. Together, they can lift a human being to the most exalted peaks of human experience from which critical analysis is excluded.

As we consider the architectural beauty produced in the world in the worship of Deity—the temples, shrines, synagogues, cathedrals, mosques or even great crosses on mountain-tops to entice worshippers to kneel in prayer at sunrise—we realize how greatly, even when indirectly, religion has enriched life.

When daylight, piercing the Five Sisters lancet windows, illumines the interior of York Cathedral, or shattered into prismatic jewels, makes Sainte-Chapelle glow like the heart of a gem, and we fall silent, or perhaps kneel, do we do obeisance to Beauty or to God? Do we need to know that the chapel was built to house the crown of thorns, or is its radiant beauty sufficient of itself to stir us and to inspire us?

Marx wrote that religion is the opiate of the poor; and let me add, they need an opiate. I watched an Arab workman enter the great mosque in Cairo. I saw him sink to his knees and prostrate himself in prayer toward Mecca—under that high, quiet dome, in the vast uncluttered central space, soft with crimson prayer rugs. Arguing from his pitiful garments to the poverty of his home, I could imagine the crowded, malodorous hovel in the shabby slums of Cairo from which he probably came. I could imagine, too, the peace he felt flooding his being, the peace of space, of enfolding vastness, of silence, in this, his spiritual home. To me, he seemed to be experiencing an esthetic release from grimness. If I could have asked him, he would doubtless have told me that he found joy in his spiritual devotions. He would have agreed that for a blissful space he had found release from the hateful sordidness of daily life. He had had a foretaste of Paradise. This benison, he would have insisted is the reward of the faithful, nor would he have understood if I had told him that he had been cradled in the arms of Beauty, twin sister to holiness, but not necessarily holiness.

Once quite alone on the streets of a foreign city, as a solitary tourist in Geneva, on a chill, gray day in early April, I suddenly experienced the panic of being isolated. Almost trembling, I slipped through an easily yielding door into the dim interior of the church of San Giovanni de Pre and the gallery of the Knights Commanders of St. John.

A kerchiefed Italian housewife left her string-bag of vegetables beside me on the bench, as she went to confession, and I, sitting there in the dim church was gradually incorporated into a shadowy procession of kindly people stretching back in my imagination through the centuries, people who had come to pray and be comforted before the altar with the six tall candles burning straight and unwaveringly. From the earliest crusader in the eleventh century bearing the sacred ashes of John the Baptist, they came, they lingered, they surrounded me, and in this drifting throng of visitors from distant ages, I found companionship. I was no longer alone. Although I had found solace in a church, had I had a religious or an esthetic experience? Or were the two fused?

In the vast-sounding phrases of the Psalms, describing how God clothes himself "with light as with a garment," or mighty mason that he is, lays the foundations of the earth "so they shall

Twin Sisters

not be moved," or ordains that "night unto night shall utter speech and day unto day show wisdom," when through such evocative magic of words man's spirit is given wings, is it great art at work, or is it religion?

And when music with the irresistible power of a great wave suspends us at a point between high heaven and black unplumbed depths of experience, who is to call the experience esthetic but not religious? One may name it with Yeats: "Eternal Beauty wandering on her way," but still admit she has her sister Holiness by the hand.

Students of history of art need also to be students of religion, and vice versa. This is universally true, although we of the West are able to appreciate it most as exemplified in Oriental art and religion. I recall a photograph of three kimona-clad women admiring a single chrysanthemum enshrined in an alcove. They sit gracefully in Japanese fashion in silent contemplation, an instance of the Oriental fusion of reverence and delight characteristic of Zen Buddhism. Even so firmly are the religious and the esthetic attitudes joined in Hindu culture as it culminates in an indissoluble bond in Yoga.

Few of us realize how much closer Aristotle's conception of the Supreme Being, the "Unmoved Mover," is to the Hindu conception of Brahma than to the Jewish and Christian conceptions of a personalized god, as a kingly figure, or a Judge, or a Father. According to Aristotle, the Supreme Being is Pure Form, perhaps best conceived as pure intellect, without taint of matter, invisible, and revealed only through his works. He is the goal of all striving. He is unseen and perfect beauty. Even as the sensible beauty of art or nature in the world about us attracts us and so moves us to action, while remaining completely at rest, just so, says Aristotle, God draws us ever toward his serene unmoved perfection. The Supreme Being in the Aristotelian scheme of things is actual, as opposed to potential, but because unlimited, exists outside of time and space. He is as immaterial as a thought.

What Aristotle calls the world of experience and Hindu thinkers call "Maya," the veil of illusion, is a temporary, ever-changing union of matter and form. The acorn becomes the oak, the child the man; cities and nations rise and fall. Only Pure Form, Aristotle's Supreme Being, the first and final cause of changing experience and the Hindu philosopher's Brahma, the all that is, the One, remain beyond time and space, indivisible, invisible, supreme.

It would have been equally unthinkable for an Aristotelean, as for a devout Hindu, to portray the creation of man as Michaelangelo has done on the great ceiling of the Sistine Chapel. No electric spark could have issued from the pointing finger of Deity, no clouds and no cherubs could have supported the mighty and august frame with its windswept beard. Adam, by his own efforts would have had to struggle from inertness toward a vast blank space on the ceiling, but the expression on his face would have been the reflection of a most glorious vision.

The aim of Hindu worship is to re-identify the worshipper with the Divine. The devotee often prepares for ecstatic union with Brahma by repeating over and over the sacred word "Om" to exclude intruding sensations that might come between him and the divine. By utter concentration and stillness, controlling his breath as well as his wandering thoughts, his heartbeats as well as his roving eyes, he enters into a sense of union with Brahma. His individual soul is linked again with the infinite source from which its bondage to the wheel of life has temporarily sundered it. In Yoga, or the yoking of the individual soul to God, the devout Brahman is freed from the limitations of self and can experience the deep significance of the Sanskrit formula *Tat tuam ast*, or "That art thou"; the blissful identity of man with his god. The union is as impersonal as that which occurs when a drop of spray falls from a cresting wave into the ocean.

Aristotle never took this mystic step. He was content to say that the use of man's intellect in thoughtful contemplation was man's highest joy, and that in such contemplation he most nearly approached the condition of deity.

Superficially, there is something in common between this Hindu doctrine of Yoga, that religious devotion is an act of merging the worshipper with the object worshipped, and Lipp's theory that an esthetic attitude is one of empathy whereby the viewer loses himself in the art object. However, Yoga and empathy are only superficially alike. Yoga is a merging with a deity, almost as has been said, as spray falls back into the vastness of the ocean from which it was briefly separated, while empathy denotes the attitude of a beholder who instead of responding to an object, as in sympathy or in loathing, feels in his own body the attitude he sees in the object of his attention. As one watches a dancer, for example, one may happily lose for a blissful space of time the sense of one's own sluggish, muscle-bound body and feel as if he is moving with the ease, the power, and the grace of the dancer. Or wandering "lonely as a cloud" with Wordsworth, he may encounter the crowd of golden daffodils and dance with them.

It is important to extend the concept of empathy beyond the sometimes narrow interpretation given to it, as evoked exclusively by muscular strains and tensions in another person or art-object such as a statue. Because we can abstract elements such as balance or strain and introject them, we can respond with empathy to many nonmuscular things, notably music.

All kite-flying human beings know that one of the most elemental and exalting responses of empathy which can be experienced is to be one not with the buffeted kite, but with the invisible surging air, the great dizzy updrafts of power, the onward and upward tugging wind. So, too, from the deck of a ship at night, stars and moon mist-shrouded, there is possible empathy with vastness itself, an empathy in which one learns the meaning of utter peace. At first, there may be a chilling awareness of the smallness of self and then a surrender to darkness and space like the blissful drifting into the security of sleep.

Thus vastness, like great music, can erase the awareness of the limitations of selfhood and immerse one in an immensity of being that defies words. When without the external aid of art or the stimulus of natural grandeur, man achieves this liberating union by mastery of himself, he deems it a religious rather than an esthetic experience. Here it is that Yoga and empathy meet, and the essence of the triumphant experience is the same.

Not all men are capable of Yoga and its austerity. For the gifted, the visible art object serves as a gate of exalted experience.

The familiar figure of Siva dancing in an arc of flame symbolizes the Hindu conception of eternal cosmic energy. It shows the ever-recurrent creation from destruction, then destruction from creation. It shows the cycles of birth and death, of death and birth, but it also speaks strongly to the beholder's sense of muscular balance translating an intellectual concept into a felt bodily state. For the Hindu of limited insight, the sensuous appeal alone undoubtedly produces empathy, and it is small wonder that Siva is so popular a Hindu god, dancing himself, as he does, into the very bodies of his followers. It is significant that Hindus say the dance takes place in Chidambaren, the center of the universe within the human heart.

There is widespread acceptance of a principle enunciated by Aristotle in his *Poetics* to the effect that by universalizing our powerful emotions through art, we are able to cope with them objectively. Thus the Greek tragedies, by purging the spectator from his personal involvement in disaster, free him from the fear that would cause him to flee from it rather than face it and from the pity that would dissolve his courage. They enable him to accept defeat, suffering, and death as the universal human lot.

A story dear to pious Buddhists illustrates the Buddha's insight in this regard. When a bereaved mother, carrying her dead son in her arms, besought the Buddha to restore her son's life, he asked her gently to bring him first a mustard seed from a household to which death had never come. The mother's fruitless search for the mustard seed brought her alleviation from rebellious grief, as she learned acquiesence to the universal law of human suffering. In this religious teaching, as in the functioning of Greek tragedy, art and religion reveal their common nature.

One of the significant aspects of esthetic response is its detachment. With detachment, the ordinary practical responses to an object are kept in abeyance. The observer is content to stare, or to listen. But neither staring nor listening, although intense, leads to further action. The object literally arrests the observer. A religious insight may halt one in like manner. Perhaps Paul had such a moment when, as Saul, he halted on the road to Damascus.

An interesting example of the union of esthetic and religious impulses occurs in a Zen painting from the 16th century A.D.

showing the Chinese-Japanese god of good-fortune, Hotei, watching two fighting cocks. He looks at them, but seems to be seeing beyond them with no interest in the outcome of their struggle. It has been suggested he is viewing the void where there is neither killer nor killed.

Writers on esthetics like Bullough and Ortega y Gasset stress a related idea which they call esthetic or psychological distance to distinguish it from spatial distance. It, in turn, is closely related to John Dewey's concept of a consummatory response in which we react to an experience as an end in itself, and not as instrumental to a further goal. Our ordinary responses are utilitarian; they serve to help us reach an objective further on. As we savor a delicious morsel, so we savor a moment of beauty. We rest in it, rejoice in it, cry out with Faust: "Tarry, thou art so fair." We inhale the rose deeply, temporarily foregoing oxygen for fragrance. We prolong the listening as the last note comes from the violin. We strain for a lingering overtone.

Undeniably, the consummatory response to beauty shares elements common also to supreme moments of religious emotion, as described in the Bible and in sacred literature of the religions of the world. The most striking common trait is a brief total absorption in the arresting object, religious or esthetic. Life reaches a full stop, content for the nonce to relinquish striving, which is ordinarily its felt essence. A sudden revelation of the sublime in nature is often described as overwhelming the observer, just as a glimpse of divine glory commonly causes men to veil their eyes or fall prone upon the earth. The falling is a consummatory response, the final gesture toward a climax that taxes man's strength to the limit.

It is not easy to decide which response, the religious or the esthetic, Shelley was describing in his "Hymn to Intellectual Beauty." Almost everyone can recall and can quote the magical opening stanza of that poem:

> The awful shadow of some unseen Power
> Floats—though unseen among us—visiting
> This various world with as inconstant wing
> As summer winds that creep from flower to flower

but not all, I think, recall the poet's personal climax, which came when the shadow of this beauty chanced to fall on him and he "shrieked and fell upon the earth in ecstasy." It was an experience strangely like that which befell Moses on a day when he was tending the sheep of his father-in-law Jethro, the priest of Midean. As told in Exodus, there in the wilderness near Mt. Horeb an angel of the Lord spoke to Moses from a bush that burned and was not consumed. Moses removed his shoes, for he knew he stood on holy ground. Of course, no unshod shepherd could follow a straying lamb over the fiery desert sand, but Moses' duty as shepherd was evidently forgotten as we see him ready to prostrate himself, staff too discarded, as he listened to a message from his God.

Speculation in regard to the nature of the response to beauty has uncovered many aspects of the nature of beauty itself. As this chapter is not a treatise on esthetics, it would be beyond its scope to mention all of them. By the same token we must note the aspects art and religion share. One of the important theories of art is that when beauty appears in a work of art, it is because the artist has achieved "significant form."

What is meant by "significant form" and how painting and sculpture in particular reflect or embody religious ideas appear in a comparison of the paintings of the masters of the Italian Renaissance and the paintings of Zen Buddhists. Zen Buddhism and Christianity are in ethical accord in that both proclaim the supremacy of human brotherhood. They are poles apart in their conceptions of deity.

The Buddha denied that he was himself a god. He was the Enlightened One, the Great Teacher, and the conception of deity he bequeathed to Zen Buddhists is the conception of a Reality so abstract it is best described in negative terms. In sharp contrast, the Christian conception of God has undergone the utmost development in personalization and humanization. God is not only Creator, King of Kings, Judge, he is a Father, able to grieve and to rejoice, not only for but with his children, the sons of men. His son Jesus Christ shares his throne and speaks to him as any son to any father.

Twin Sisters

It is true that later followers of Buddha elevated him to the status of a god, but that was not his original teaching and that is not the doctrine that inspires Zen art. Zen holds true to the concept of the abstract deity, whereas Christian art has been nourished by the Christian and Jewish doctrine of deity as most truly known in human terms.

For Christians, the second person of the Trinity, "very God of very God" that he is, is also a perfect human being. We celebrate his nativity, we go into mourning on the day of his death, annually re-enact the story of his passion, rejoice greatly on the spring morning when still in human form he rises Godlike from the dead.

The Christian art that fills the galleries of our Western World with madonnas and scenes of the crucifixion is an art of strongly human appeal. The holy infant which Mary holds is an appealing child, and the thin circlet of his halo cannot lend distance to the immediate appeal of his adorable babyhood. The art which depicts his humiliation, suffering, and death presents him to us as a fellow human being for whom we feel the deepest sympathy. It is an art of little distance.

As Buddhism as a religion has not humanized its deity, there is no temptation for the artist to do so. Instead, a canvas inspired by Zen Buddhism has usually an eloquent emptiness in the misty center. An insignificant and obscurely drawn human being may appear in a corner foreground. The other brush strokes will suggest a rock or a waterfall. There may be a hint of birds in flight, but they are unimportant. They are Maya, the veil of illusion that hides reality.

Buddhists with their great leader Buddha, Islamic religionists with their prophet Mohammed, and Hindus with their succession of heroic leaders have a great advantage over the followers of the Jewish and Christian religions because they have no need to humanize their gods. Upon their religious leader born human, they can hang their legends. They can portray their exploits in verbal or pictorial art and merely enhance their virtue by so doing. Of course, they risk the opposite danger to that encountered by Christian art. They may elevate their leaders to a state of divinity, while Christian art tends to dilute the majesty of divinity by making it human, all too human.

Other religions have humanized their gods, but none more completely than Christianity and Judaism, whose Jehovah walked with Adam in the Garden of Eden in the cool of the evening. The Greek gods were, it is true, the embodiment of human potentialities, but they had great distance because they were not personalities with life histories, so much as bundles of abstract human qualities and emotions housed in magnificent human forms.

It is possible, though I would be rash to proclaim it as true, that the ancient Egyptians may have given their gods animal heads on human bodies in order to keep them divine and different from men. Or it may be simply that in their jackal-headed, ram-headed, hawk-headed sculptured divinities an earlier animal-worship mingled with sun worship. In either case, the effect was the same, their gods were dehumanized. His worshippers cannot empathize with hawk-headed Horus any more than Babylonian followers of the true and mighty Shamash could feel at one with the glorious disc of the life-giving sun.

When our Stonehenge ancestors built Stonehenge to entrap the rising sun within the angle of their monolithic stones on midsummer morning, it is still a question whether they built as astronomers and mathematicians or as sun worshippers. But to us today, they seem to have erected a miracle of art. With flawless engineering skill they enshrined the moment of the year which held for them surpassing significance. In his *Three Lectures on Aesthetics* Bernard Bosanquet wrote in 1915: "The point of the esthetic attitude lies in the adequate fusion of body and soul, where the soul is feeling and the body its expression, without residue on either side." This, I contend, might equally well pass for a definition of the truly religious experience. If so, Stonehenge is both a religious and an artistic triumph.

No writer that I know has more subtly analyzed and limited the function of what he calls "the sensuous surface" of the esthetic experience than the late David Prall. He says that as we leave the surface of sound and sight and other sensuous experience or-

Twin Sisters

ganized by form, to plunge deeply into the ocean of meanings and broad relationships, we no longer have an esthetic experience but a new type of experience. It is possible that this other type of experience to which Prall said the esthetic can lead is religious.

Like the world revealed to us by Jacques-Yves Cousteau, it is a world of awe and wonder, of undreamed-of delicacy and terror, a world of challenge.

If at life's end we are cradled into peace by encircling arms, it does not greatly matter whether they are the arms of art or of her sister religion, since beauty and holiness are in such deep accord. Either can ease the way into the sleep, "Too deep for waking, and for dreams too deep." Either can lift man's spirit to heights where he glimpses the sublime.

Historians of Chinese art, such as Ludwig Bachhofen, agree that Buddhism brought to China the idea that art is ancillary to religion; and in painting, sculpture, and architecture its role is to make manifest the divine. In this service Chinese art has certainly achieved its greatness, a greatness we are sometimes too untutored to grasp.

Philosophers of art, who have considered profoundly the relationship between religion and art, have had memorable things to say. Roger Fry said both demand the exercise of certain capacities of human nature that are ends in themselves. Both, for instance, involve the employment of imaginative elements without which living is a meager experience. "When we live at all," wrote Santayana, "We live in the imagination." Moreover, it is possible that Clive Bell's theory of art as significant form, which we considered briefly, applies beyond the field of art in its limited context. It may apply to that enriched experience of life which is essentially religious, in which the observant eye finds highest values coexistent and interdependent.

Deity is not far distant, nor yet totally unknown, when we kneel in the presence of beauty. From the grasp of a hero's hand, we gain superhuman strength and from listening for the dying words of the saints and martyrs of the world, we hear the syllables of God's justice. What men may scoffingly assure us are dissolving mirages may prove to be the shining pinnacles of reality.

An undeniable appeal to Theosophy lies in its grasp of the problem of this chapter. By its firm assertion of the "Ancient Wisdom" that all reality is the partial manifestation of "Om" and in addition a Pythagorean conviction that the inner being of "Om" is best seen in the orderly relationship and patterns of numbers forever existing, it is evident that laws of harmony in music and laws of proportion in architecture, as well as laws of unity in the drama, are not merely aesthetic canons. They are also divine.

"Om," essentially and eternally unknowable, can yet be approached in thought as an ultimate unity expressing a self in manifold ways. In every art we glimpse an aspect. In every natural object we can catch a hint of its always-ordered and patterned being.

For a theosophist an experience of beauty is indeed a revelation of divinity. It is confirmation of what Emerson called the "Beautiful Necessity" of ultimate being.

CHAPTER XVI

Postscript

In every profession where the disciplined minds of men seek to find and to follow the intricate patterns of reality, reverence emerges. Civil engineers as well as historians seek truth. Psychiatrists as well as astronomers honor laws. As cultural anthropologists, working with scientific objectivity, reassemble the fragmented past into a meaningful whole, that whole takes on an aura of awe and sublimity.

It may have been true that in the yesterdays of time enlightened ones were a special priestly few: the Buddhas, Isaiahs, Zoroasters, Mohammeds who set themselves apart to meditate on truth and gain revelation.

Today, bit by bit, revelation comes to men bending over microscopes, peering into telescopes, heating test tubes, growing cultures, deciphering records, putting together bits and pieces, adding up figures, projecting diagrams, manipulating symbols. It comes to an army of hard-working, scientific toilers in the laboratories, libraries, and work-sites of the world.

They are building for their fellowmen visions so stupendous we should not take them as casually as we often do. Like Moses before the burning bush, we should remove our shoes and say: "Surely this place we stand on is hallowed ground."

Alfred Noyes has summed it all up for us:

> What is all science then
> But pure religion ......
>
> . . . .
>
> A boundless task in whose infinitude
> Abides our hope, and our eternal joy.

What more, Goethe asked in one of his occasional poems, does man need than the assurance he has from divine nature (*Gott-Natur*) of its unswerving adherence to order? Down the ages prophets and poets have urged us to follow the "gleam." Tennyson wrote:

> O young mariner
> Down to the haven
> Call your companions
> Launch your vessel
> And crowd your canvas,
> And, ere it vanishes
> Over the margin,
> After it, follow it,
> Follow the gleam.

Speaking of the universal role of humanity, Masefield wrote of being "in quest of that one beauty God put me here to find."

In the preface to "Plays Pleasant and Unpleasant," George Bernard Shaw wrote: "There is only one religion, though there are a hundred versions of it."

In "What I believe" in the *Forum* for October, 1930, Albert Einstein wrote: "The most beautiful thing we can experience is the mysterious. It is the source of all true art and science," and, I would add, with what seems to me the acquiescence of Goethe, Tennyson, Masefield, Shaw, Einstein, and countless others, "religion."

When it comes to being truly religious one could not be in better state than to be able in all sincerity, to echo the statement of the wise Buddha "I am awake"—awake to the mysterious but eternally self-revealing, the challenging and elusive universe, the satisfying universe of awesome beauty and order, forever beyond complete knowing, in which nonetheless we are at home.

Index

Absolute, the, 93
Absolute perfection, 126
Absolutes, self-contradictory, 101
Acorns and magic transformation, 40
Acquiescence to universal law, 172
Adam and Eve, 36, 148
Adon, 57
Adversary, 92
Affair, Doom's Day, 6-7
Affinity, 145
Ahasuerus, 134
Ahriman, 5
Ahura-Mazda, against Ahriman, 5, 7, 16, 19, 77, 95-98, 102
Aiken, Conrad, quoted, 158
Alexander, Samuel, Deity as an emergent, 163
Alexander the Great, 81
All that is, 159
Allah, 12, 92, 98
Amanita muscario, 40
Ambrosia, 37-38
Amon-Ra, 143
"Ancient Wisdom," 178
Angels
    Angelic roles in Islamic belief, 21-22
    Augustine's definition, 13
    Church fathers' attitude, 18
    guardian angels, 21-22, 138
    for children, 18
    Mohammed, 21
    Moroni, 22-23
    Old Testament accounts, 18
    robes, 18
    Sadducees, 18
    Zoroastrianism, 19-23
Animal heads of Egyptian gods, 176
Animism, 25-26, 28, 31, 33-34, 117
    and concept of Yang and Yin, 94-97
Anti-Christ, 133
Anti-Semitism, aided by miracle and morality plays, 132-33
Apple, 36
Appollinarian heresy, 135
Aquinas, Thomas, 19, 108, 133
Archangels, name and duties, 17. *See also* Angels
Aristotle, doctrine of purging, 172
Art and religion, 168-69
Artemis, 118-19, 122, 139, 140
Aryan migration, 47-48
Asclepius, 81
Aton, 143
Atys, 58
Augustine, 144
Aztecs, 118

Bab, 155
Bachhofen, Ludwig, 177-78
Bahai doctrine, 159
Bahaism, 154-55
Baha-i-ullah, 155
Balder, 66, 101
Barzini, Luigi, quoted, 143-44
Beans, 43
Beauty, twin sister to holiness, 168
Bell, Clive, 177
Benedict, Ruth, 83
Bigots, 135, 151-52

"Book of the Dead," 4, 44, 59
Bosanquet, Bernard, quoted, 176
Brahma (or Brahman)
 creator, 9
 the inscrutable ground of being, 86-88, 106
"Bridge of the Separator," 5-6, 98
Brooke, Rupert, quoted, 88
Browne, Lewis, quoted, 62
Bruno, Giordano, 137
Bryant, William Cullen, quoted, 78
Buddha, 31-32, 64-66, 75, 112, 160
Buddhism
 teachings, 89-91
 two sects, Mahayana and Hinayana, 65-66
Burke, Edmund, 166
Bynner, Witter, 74

Carroll, Lewis, 35, 101
Cherubim (or cherubs, or cheribim), appearance, 15-17
Chippewa Indians, version of the flood, 49
Children, need of parents' clarity on vital issues, 164
Christian art, 175
Chu-Hsi, 95
Civil marriage, 145
Common law marriage, 145
Comte, Auguste, 161-63
Confucius, 68
Confucianism, 9, 94-95
Conjuration, 107-8
Consummatory responses, 175
Crusaders, 130-33
Cult
 of Mithras, 98
 of Virgin, 141
Cyclical world conflagration, 9-10

Dance, as prayer, 110-11
Daniel's food habits, 43
Dante, 158
David's dance before the Ark, 113
Deity, concept of, and art, 175

Demeter, 37-38
Detachment in art and religion, 172-73
Dewey, John, on learning, 70
DNA code, and resurrection, 71
Doom's Day, Zoroaster's version, 6
Dunham, Katherine, 126

Ecstasy, religious, 166, 174
Edwards, Jonathan, 102, 125
Eight-fold pathway, 91
Einstein, Albert, quoted, 180
Eliot, George, quoted, 162
Emerson, Ralph Waldo, quoted, 10, 178
Empathy, 170-71
Emperor worship, 82-83
Epicurus, 122
Esthetic and religious experience, easily confused, 168
Eternal recurrence, 101
Eucharist, 44-46

Faith as supreme value, 150
Fanaticism, 152
Father, 141
Fenris-wolf, 101
Fiske, John, quoted, 3
Flood, 47-48, 51-52
Food mystique, 35, 44
Four noble truths, 91
Frazer, Sir James, quoted, 129
Free-floating anxiety, 163
Freud, Sigmund, 142-44
Fromm, Erich, quoted, 147-48
Fry, Roger, 177

Gabriel, 17, 20-21, 98. *See also* Archangel
Gautama Siddharta, 63-65, 85-87
Genius (genii) 27, 30-31. *See also* Angels
Gestalt psychology and Taoism, 75
Gilgamesh Epic (and flood), 53
God, 77, 92, 119
Goethe, Johann Wolfgang von, quoted, 180

Index

Golden Bough, The, quoted, 129
Golden Rule, as stated in nine religions, 151
Golems, 28
"Great Stone Face" (of New Hampshire), recognized as "the Sky-Father," 49-50
Grensted, Canon, quoted, 152
Guardian angels. *See* Angels

Hanukkah, 115
Hazel nuts, 37
Hecate (Artemis), 122
Heretic, 135-36
Holi, 112
Holy Sepulcher, 131
Home, Roman feeling of its sanctity, 31
Household gods, shrines in Bangkok, 31
Housman, A. E., quoted, 124
Huitzitopochtli, 117

Ibsen, Henrik, quoted, 101
Imam, 155-56
Immaculate Conception, 140
Inquisition, 134-36
Islam, 99, 175

James, William, quoted, 105, 160
Jannissaries, 129
Jatakas, 90
Jehovah, 28, 92
Jesus, 137, 140
Jewish calendar, 113-16
Jihads, 131
Jinns (jenni), 28
Judgment Day, 3-12, 21, 162
Jung, Carl Gustav, quoted, 84

Ka, 4, 44
Kant, Immanuel, innate patterns of intellect, 69-70, 153-54
Kapiolani, 123-24
Kara shi shi, 33. *See also* seraphim
Karma, 3, 71, 85-86, 89
Kinds of knowledge, 152-53

King Solomon's ring, 134
Kismet, 75
Koran, 21, 98-99, 135, 156, 165

Lao Tzu, 9, 74
Lares and penates, 29-32
Lethe, 39
Li, 72, 95
Lipp, Theodor, 170-71
Living goddesses of Nepal, 84
Logos, 76
Loki, 100
Longfellow, Henry Wadsworth, quoted 18-19, 76, 106
Lotus
  buds, 39
  flowers, 48
Lucretius, 122-25
Luther, Martin, 159

Magic, gadgets, prayer wheels, flags, 103
Mahavira, 62, 112
Mana, 27
Marriage, 144-49
Masefield, John, quoted, 180
Matter, redefined, 71
Matthew, St., 108
Maya, 9, 169
McConnell, James, experiment with flat-worms, 35-36
Mill, John Stuart, 152
Millennium, and final judgment Day, 11-12
Milton, John, quoted, 15, 17, 119
Mirza, 155
Mithras (Mithra or Mitra), 61-63, 73, 77, 98
Mizpah, 107
Mohammed, 20-21, 98
Mohmud, 128-29
Molech, 118
Moral bookkeeper, 159
Moroni, 22-23
Moses, 17, 174
Moslem husband, 146

Moslem prayer, quoted, 110
Munis, holy men, 42
Mystery cults, 59-61

Nativity of Jesus, 63
Nectar and ambrosia, 37, 54
Nicea, Council of, 135
Noncritical thinking, 163-64
Norse version of problem of evil, 100
Noyes, Alfred, quoted, 2, 179

Oath of clearance, 4-5
Obligatory prayer, 108
Odin, 77, 100, 102
Odor of sanctity, 134
Oldenbourg, Zoe, 129-30
Om, 78, 170, 178
Origin, 108
Orthodoxy, 157
Osiris, 4, 59
Otto, Rudolph, 160

Paine, Tom, quoted, 166
Pallas Athena, 139
Parsee, 92
Passover, 115
Pattern
  basic, 69
  as creation, 67
  happiness as conformity to pattern, 68
  intellect, 68
  Kant's a priori, 68
  Pythagoras, mathematical patterns, 69
  science's search for pattern, 68
Paul, on marriage, 146-47
Perpetual chant, 105
Persephone, 38
Peyote, 41-42. *See also* Lotus, 48
Pilgrimages, 130
Poseidon, 51, 120-21, 123
Positivism, 161-62
Prall, David, 176-77
Prayer:
  agnostic prayers, 103
  Augustine on, 103
  bodily attitudes, 109-10
  boxes, 103
  Buddhist prayer, 104
  Moslem, 110
  petitionary, 104
  restriction, 111
  wheels, 104
Prenuptial intercourse, 146
Primitive thinking, 26. *See also* Animism
Prometheus, 51, 121-22
Pure form and Brahma, 170
Purim, 115
Pythagoras, 43

Ramadan, 112-13
Reincarnation, 8, 90
Religion and esthetics confused, 167
Religion as sublimated sex drive, 142
Religion of Humanity, 162
Religious fanaticism, 128
Revelation, 179
Rexroth, Kenneth, questioned re personal God behind Brahman, 87
Rita (Dharma), cosmic patterns, 73
Rivalry between religions and ethics, 150
Rosh Hashanah, 114
Rosaries, 106

Sabbath, 114
Sacred rites, 111-12
Sacrifice, 45
Sago-King Yu, 52
Saladin, 131
Salat, 108-9
Santayana, George, quoted, 177
Satan, 17, 19, 91-93
Schism, 130
Self-annihilation, 63
Seraphim, 14-15

Index

Shades, 22
Shakers, 28
Shavuos, 116
Shaw, George Bernard, quoted, 180
Shelley, Percy Bysshe, quoted, 173-74
Significant form, 174
Sin, 156-57
Siva, 9, 172
Smith, George, 52-53
Smith, Huston, quoted, 110
Soma (also Laoma), 40-41
Sophocles, on the eternity of moral laws, 73
Soul, 8, 95
Special saints, 23. *See also* Angels
Spinoza, Benedictus (or Baruch), 159-60
Spirits, many forms, 27
State Shinto, 83-84
Stoicism, 74-75
Stonehenge, 176
Struggle of good and evil central to Zoroastrianism, 95-96
Sublimation in religion, 142
Sublime, the, 168-69
Succos, 114

Taboos, of food, 143-44
Tamerlane, 80
Tammus, 55-56
Tao, 74
Tao Te Ching, quoted, 74
Taoism, 9, 74-75, 109
Tauroboleum, 60-61
Temple prostitute, 139
Tennyson, Alfred Lord, quoted, 125, 180
Teraphim as idols, 29
Theosophy, 157, 178
Thor, 100, 102
Three baskets of wisdom, 9
Torah, 116
Trachtenberg, Joshua, 133
Transcendental belief, 154
Trent, Council of, 145
Tribunal of Judgment, 7
Truly religious, 180
Tutelary gods of Japan, 32
Tyr (or Tui), 100

Ultimate Being, 89
Union with Brahma, 170
Unknowable deity, effect on art, 175
Unmoved movers compared with Brahma, 169
Urban II (Pope), 130

Values confused, religious and esthetic, 166
Values: ethical conduct vs. faith, 150
Vastness and empathy, 171
Vedas, 85-86, 89
Vicarious satisfaction, 142
Vishnu, 9, 54
Votive candles, as part of prayer, 105
Vow, more than a prayer, 105

Walum-olum, 47, 50
Well of wisdom, 39
Wembridge, Eleanore, quoted, 149
Whitehead, Alfred North, quoted, 91
Woman, 138-49
Woolley, Leonard, 48
Wordsworth, William, quoted, 24

Xenophanes, 88

Yahweh, 119
Yang and Yin, 93-95, 102
Yeats, William Butler, quoted, 169
Yoga, 168, 170-71
Yom Kippur, 114

Zen Buddhism, 75, 163-65
Zeno, 10, 73
Zeus, 51, 121, 122, 139, 177
Zoroaster (or Zarathustra), 5,-7, 40, 92, 96-97